Creative
TRIANGLES FOR QUILTERS

JANET B. ELWIN

Chilton Book Company
Radnor, Pennsylvania

Designed by Anthony Jacobson
Line drawings by Carolyn Turcio-Gilman
Color photography by David Caras

Manufactured in the United States of America

The following trademark terms have been mentioned in this book:
    Clover Chaco-Liner marker
    Clover pins
    Omni-Grid ruler
    Pfaff Creative 1475
    Q-Snap plastic frame

If you are interested in a quarterly newsletter about creative uses of the sewing machine and serger, edited by Robbie Fanning, write to *The Creative Machine,* P.O. Box 2634-B, Menlo Park, CA 94026.

Library of Congress Cataloging-in-Publication Data

Elwin, Janet B.
    Creative triangles for quilters / Janet B. Elwin
        p.   cm.
    Includes index.
    ISBN 0-8019-8477-7 (pbk.)
    1. Patchwork—Patterns.   2. Quilting—Patterns.   3. Triangle.
    I. Title.
    TT835.E468   1995
    746.46—dc20   94-49350
                                                              CIP

1 2 3 4 5 6 7 8 9 0   4 3 2 1 0 9 8 7 6 5

To my children,
Mark, Toby, and Lea,
who loved me enough to let me grow.

Thank you.

Contents

Acknowledgments   viii

1 Introduction   1

2 Drawing a 60° Triangle   7

Drawing a 60° Triangle   7
Enlarging and Reducing the Triangle   8
Using the 1" Grid   8

3 Piecing Triangles and Other Hints   11

Making Templates   11
Marking and Cutting Cloth   12
Piecing   14
Borders   16
Ironing   16
Quilting   16
Binding the Quilt   18

4 Basic Triangle Quilts   21

A Quilted Triptych   21
    Triptych I and *Wallhanging I*   22
    Triptych IV and *Wallhanging IV*   24
    Triptych XVI and *Wallhanging XVI*   27
Variations on a Theme: Full-Size Quilts   31
    Basic Triangle Quilt   31
    Medallion Quilt, Queen   32
    Medallion Quilt, King   35
    Vertical Triangle Quilt   37

5 Contemporary Quilts   43

A Year in the Life of My Tree   43
Lavender Blue   49

6 All-Pieced Fan and Dresden Plates   63

Special Techniques Used in Fan and Dresden Plate Quilts   64
Green Fans   66
Blue Dresden Plates   68
Return to Dresden   71
Necktie Quilt   75

7 Curves   85

Windy Way   86
Whirlwind   90
Pond Lilies   92

8 Fractured Triangles   101

Hichinin Schimai   103
After the Hunt   110

9 More Triangles   119

Fly-A-Way   119
Hot Flashes   123

10 Wrap Up   133

Index   135

Acknowledgments

Always to Bud for his love, support, and never-ending encouragement.

To Carolyn Turcio-Gilman for her beautiful artwork, her genius at interpreting my drawings, her skill at the computer, and her confidence in me and this project.

To Pfaff for making a sewing machine with all that creativity built right in.

To David Caras for the wonderful photography.

And to all my students who keep me on my toes, always asking just the right questions to challenge me.

And again to Dave and Bill, you were there once more.

Introduction

Several years ago, I purchased an art book containing a copy of a Renoir painting that I had been looking for. The book contained about 20 different frameable prints featuring works by many of the Impressionists, including Monet. I had always loved Monet and I already had several books featuring much of his work. But this new book gave me the chance to study several other artists as well. I noticed one technique, which several of the Impressionists used, that particularly intrigued me—pointillism. Instead of brushing on strokes of paint, the artist dotted bits of color on a canvas. Up close, I didn't care for this effect, but, when viewed from a short distance away, the overall impression created by the painting was quite beautiful. It reminded me a lot of how quiltmakers approach their work. They take many bits and pieces of cloth and put them all together to create an overall image. This technique also related to what I had been trying to do: create an overall impression rather than starkly defined images.

I have developed an approach for creating impressionistic quilt designs with triangles, especially the 60° triangle. I combine the 60° triangle with a monochromatic color scheme (many shades, tints, and patterns of one color) to create a visual picture or impression of a place I have seen or an occasion I want to remember. For instance, when making a quilt with a lot of sky, instead of cutting one large piece of blue, I take two or three shades (you can use many more) and cut them into triangles. This blending of fabrics gives a mottled effect which is more like a real sky. Take a good look at the sky. It is really many shades of colors. By using fabrics of several shades of the same color, you too can achieve a more realistic, mottled effect. Triangles work very nicely because they fit together so neatly.

Blending the fabrics also gives you, the designer, much more flexibility with the way you use your fabrics, and the outcome is often a softer and more sophisticated look. This is possible because you're using fabrics in new ways. You can combine several pieces that might not ordinarily go together by cutting them into small triangles, blending the fabric colors, or fracturing the cut triangles (see Chapter 8). I have used a lot of odd pieces (I don't know what I was thinking when I purchased some of these "dogs") in the quilts in this book that really wouldn't have been very attractive if I had used them in large chunks. You can soften the look of geometric patterns by using many triangles rather than one large one; look at *Triptychs I, IV,* and *XVI* in Chapter 4. I think the more fabrics in a triangle, the softer the look. You can make a simple pattern much more sophisticated by using many triangles, blending fabrics, or fracturing the triangles. Look at the *Australian Seven Sisters* and *Hichinin Schimai* quilts in Chapter 8. These designs add sophistication to traditional patterns with their skillful use of fabrics in the fracturing technique. Also, the use of two blended fabrics in the backgrounds of *Hichinin Schimai* (Chapter 8) and *Blue Dresden Plates* (Chapter 6) softens the visual image in these quilts. I use this technique of blending monochromatic fabrics in many aspects of my quilting, as you will see in the quilts featured in this book. When I use the term "blended" in the following chapters, I'm referring to this technique.

I like to purchase, beg, borrow, or steal my fabrics, most of which are prints. I use a wide range of fabric prints, from micro-prints to big, bold splashy designs. There are times when I don't have the exact amount of fabric in a color I need, yet by putting together several fabrics that are closely related in color (blended), I can produce either enough of the color I need or the overall image I am looking for. As you read through the fabric requirements for the different quilts in this book, you will notice that I repeatedly call for blended (very closely related) fabrics. In many cases, you will not notice the subtle blending of the backgrounds when you first look at the photos of the quilts in this book. For instance, look at *Triptych XVI* in Chapter 4, *Blue Dresden Plates* in Chapter 6, and *Hot Flashes* in Chapter 9. Perhaps you didn't realize at first glance that the alternate triangle in *Triptych XVI* is actually 16 closely related prints of the same color family (monochromatic) instead of one print.

Why do I insist on blending my fabrics and why do I encourage you to try it? There are different reasons behind different quilt patterns. In *Triptych XVI,* I had a lot of fabrics, but didn't want to use the large triangle template to alternate these fabrics with my main color. By breaking down the template into a much smaller triangle, I was able to use all my coordinating prints and achieve a much softer look. With the background in *Blue Dresden Plates,* I used two blended tan prints to give a shadow effect which also is a little softer. This softening effect is easy to achieve. Instead of using a white background in a quilt, try combining white and muslin. Another method is to buy white fabrics at several stores. Most likely they will be different shades of white and will be especially interesting to the eye when put together.

Fabric blending is a good technique for portraying trees in quilts. Again, look at nature. In the summer, a tree does not appear as merely one shade of green. The leaves are many and piled one on top of the other in bunches. This creates shadows and color changes. Instead of making a tree with one shade of green, try using several shades and one simple shape—the triangle. This will create an impressionistic image similar to the shading in real trees. To see how this looks, see the quilts *A Year in the Life of My Tree* in Chapter 5 and *After the Hunt* in Chapter 8.

Blending does not have to be complicated. The background triangles of *Hichinin Schimai,* Chapter 8, show a very simple way to blend by using two closely related triangles instead of a big bold diamond. This can be taken one step further by blending three fabrics, as I did in the background of *Hot Flashes* (Chapter 9). In both of these quilts I have softened the impact of a lot of background by using closely blended fabrics and triangles or variations of the triangle. This technique makes the quilt pattern the focus of attention while allowing the background to softly complement the design.

The blending of fabrics is one way to achieve a sophisticated soft look in many of our quilts. The use of the 60° triangle is a bonus that makes the quilt even more interesting to look at. Most of us start quilting by making sampler "blocks." We tend to gravitate toward designs based on simple blocks. The end result is blocks set together side by side, row by row, as shown in Figure 1-1.

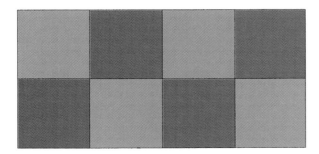

Figure 1-1 Typical quilt block arrangement

In 60° quilts, the triangles are stitched together in rows with the fabric design alternating (see Figure 1-2). This gives a mosaic look that I find particularly appealing.

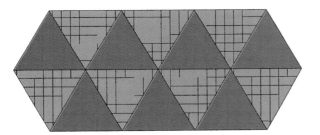

Figure 1-2 Quilt "block" arrangement using 60° triangles

Notice the difference between the star created from 60° triangles, which form a hexagon (Figure 1-3), and the star created from 45° triangles forming a square (Figure 1-4). I find the look of the 60°-triangle star much more intriguing—it has more movement. In addition, quilts using 60° triangles look much more complicated than they really are because of the way the pieces fit into one another.

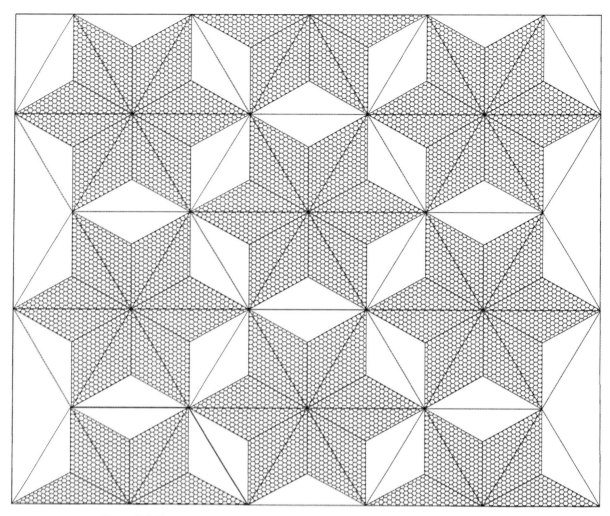

Figure 1-3 Stars created from 60°-triangle blocks

The simple triangle shape makes beautiful quilts that can showcase your fabulous fabric collection. It doesn't take quilters very long to amass a fabric collection, even if it is all leftovers from a first quilt with a few pieces added here and there. We need never feel guilty about collecting fabric. Fabric is the most important tool of our trade. It is ever so much easier to have a brilliant idea for a quilt when all the fabrics are at hand. Well, almost all of them. I have also found that fabric is a great souvenir. There is no need to justify our buying habits. We see what we need and we need what we see.

New quilters don't need hundreds of pieces of fabric to create beautiful quilts, however. I can remember having an idea for a quilt, then buying exactly what I needed for that project, usually two or three yards of several fabrics. I didn't have the room or the inclination to collect many different fabrics for a single quilt. Well, that didn't last very long. Soon I had fabrics left over from each project. Before long, I began seeing fabrics that I just couldn't live without. Very soon, my little tiny sewing room had many bits and pieces. Over the years, I have changed my buying habits from collecting two to three yards of one piece to buying lots of smaller pieces of many fabrics.

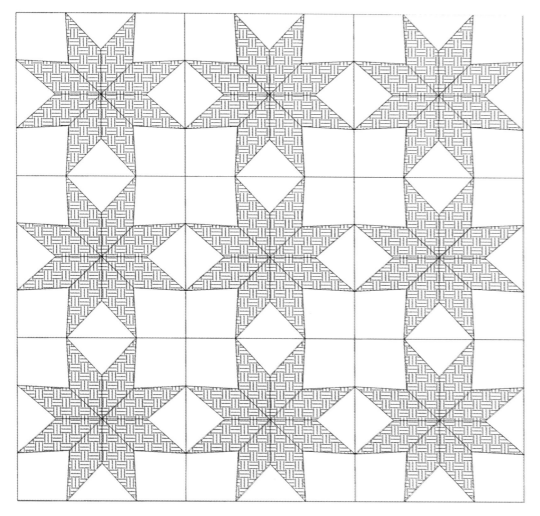

Figure 1-4 Stars created from 45°-triangle blocks

I have been collecting fabrics for a long time. I have learned to take advantage of every opportunity to use as many fabrics as I can in every quilt. Even though these are called "scrap quilts," the scraps aren't randomly arranged. Instead they're carefully organized. Most of the fabrics are new or left over from another project. I do, however, haunt thrift shops, save my favorite old clothes, and even take the shirts off people's backs. I use it all, from 100% cotton to anything that is the right color, print, or texture. I am always eager to mix fabrics and use up stuff that I have been saving for years. That way, I can then replenish my stock.

Whatever you do with your fabric collection, don't worry about using every single piece you buy. Don't worry about running out of that perfect piece you wanted for your quilt. I have found I get the most creative ideas when I run out of fabrics. You'll find a solution. Be creative! Eventually you will find the right quilt for those two yards you couldn't live without ten years ago. You will find the perfect coordinating fabric to work into the quilt that is half done even though you ran out of fabric.

All of these things, from love of fabrics to the visual enjoyment of quilts, is what turned me on to triangles and the making of what I call organized scrap quilts.

You'll find that triangles are easy to work with. They have a great look. They also combine to form an image that appears more complex than it really is. That last statement may seem like a contradiction, but when you make a simple-shaped triangle quilt with wonderful fabrics, people often assume it is quite complex. So, dazzle your friends.

In this book I want to share a few of the quilts I've made with basic triangles as well as some with designs created within the triangle shape. One of the quilts (*Windy Way*, Chapter 7) is made using only two fabrics. Some are made with several fabrics, but many have 50 or more (great for those who have fabric stashes)! Whatever your fancy, whether you like scrap quilts or quilts using a limited selection of fabric, take advantage of the overall diagram of each quilt. Put tracing paper over the diagram and trace the outline. Then put in your own colors to give a personal touch to the idea. If you prefer, go straight to the fabric; make a miniature paste-up sample in fabrics you like. Or, simply start cutting and do the layout on a flannel wall (as described below) or the floor.

A flannel wall can be done in several ways. Actually, I don't have one (no wall space), so I just lay out a piece of flannel on the floor. But then you are looking at your quilt at an angle and, of course, it can't stay there very long if you have animals, little kids, or general foot traffic. If you have a blank wall or can cover an already hanging quilt (I do this also), just push pin a good size piece of flannel (some people actually use cotton batting, which works great) into the wall. The flannel needs to be quite a bit larger than your finished quilt size because your pieces will include seam allowance and you need plenty of room to lay the pieces on the flannel side by side. Lots of quilters like a flannel wall because they then can view the finished quilt before sewing it together. If they don't like the look of a piece of fabric or placement of the fabric, they can change it around before they start to sew.

I have found these quilts easy to sew, and you will, too. Don't just look at the photograph or the diagram. Read through the directions one step at a time and try following the sewing sequences as you go. I find it much clearer to work step by step, rather than trying to absorb all the directions before I begin. The beauty of 60°-angle quilts is that they can look breathtakingly complicated but be strikingly simple to sew. It's all in the angle!

Drawing a 60° Triangle

Drawing a 60° Triangle

TOOLS REQUIRED

30°-60°-90° Drafting Triangle, available at art supply stores
Sharp Pencil
Plain White Paper
Eraser

This couldn't be easier. Fold the paper in half and crease it to create a center line.

Tape the paper to a drafting mat or table.

Line the drafting triangle up to the center crease as shown, and trace the outline of the long edge and the bottom edge. Flip the triangle to the other side of the crease and trace the long and bottom edge again.

Figure 2-1 Paper with center crease

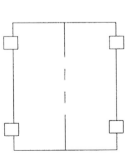

Figure 2-2 Paper taped to table

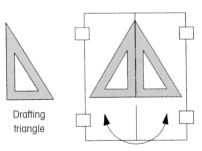

Figure 2-3 Drawing a 60° triangle

Drafting triangle

Enlarging and Reducing the Triangle

If the triangle needs to be larger than the drafting triangle, just extend the side lines from the top point. Slide the drafting triangle downward along one side line and continue drawing until the long edge is the length you want. Flip the drafting triangle to the other half of the paper and do the same thing. Make sure that both extended sides are the same length. Redraw the line across the bottom.

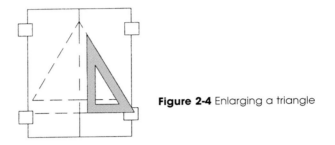

Figure 2-4 Enlarging a triangle

To make a triangle that's smaller than the drafting triangle, prepare the paper, line up the drafting triangle along the crease, and draw the long edge the length that you want. Then slide the drafting triangle upward along the line just drawn until the bottom of the triangle meets the end of the line. Draw across the bottom edge of the triangle to the center crease. Flip the drafting triangle to the other half of the paper and do the same thing. Make sure that both shortened sides are the same length.

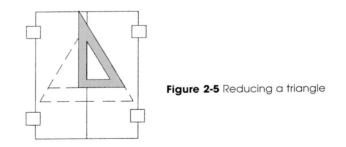

Figure 2-5 Reducing a triangle

Using the 1" Grid

To use the 1" grid in Figure 2-6 to make accurate templates of a 60° triangle, follow these steps.

1. Determine the size (length of each side) of triangle you want.

2. Put tracing paper or see-through template plastic over the grid.

3. Using a ruler, trace the grid lines that form the size triangle you want. This is shown in Figure 2-7 on page 10.

Figure 2-6 A 60° triangle grid of 1" triangles

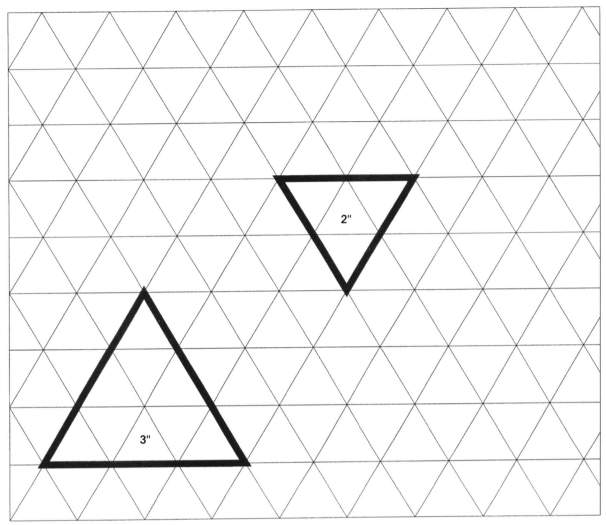

Figure 2-7 Using the 1" grid to make a 2" and a 3" 60° triangle

This template will be the finished size, so don't forget to add seam allowance (see Chapter 3). The grid can be used for any 60° angle shape, such as a diamond or hexagon (see Template K in Chapter 8 and Template C in Chapter 9), and is useful for designing 60° angle quilts.

3

Piecing Triangles and Other Hints

Making Templates

There are two ways that I like to make templates. The first method is the one that works best for beginning quilters. It's also the one I always use when making the first block of a new design. This book includes patterns that can be made with or without a seam allowance. When making either kind of template, be sure to use a fine point pen or pencil so that the line thickness doesn't distort the measurement.

MAKING TEMPLATES WITH NO SEAM ALLOWANCES

1. Disregard the solid lines on the pattern.

2. Trace along the dotted line directly from the book onto template plastic or cardboard. The dotted line indicates the stitching line.

3. Using scissors reserved just for paper and plastic, cut the templates along the dotted line you have traced.

4. Open your fabric and place it face down. Put the template on top of the wrong side and trace around the template. Leave at least ½" between traced shapes so you can add the seam allowance when cutting.

5. By eye, cut ¼" around each template shape to give the seam allowance.

This method will give you a precise line to stitch on, assuring accuracy. Another reason I like this method: if your block does not come out, you can just turn to the reverse side of the fabric and check your stitching lines.

MAKING TEMPLATES WITH SEAM ALLOWANCES

1. For this method you need to use a pattern that has the seam allowance included (the patterns in this book include ¼" seam allowances, which are indicated by solid lines). Before tracing the pattern, check your sewing machine to assure that the gauge on the machine is the same as the ¼" on the pattern by taking the following steps.

▼ Make a template from tracing paper, including both dotted lines and solid lines. Be sure to use a fine point pen or pencil so that the line thickness doesn't distort the measurement.

▼ Cut the tracing paper template along the solid line.

▼ Insert the tracing paper template under the needle in your machine.

▼ Put the needle down into the dotted line, then put the presser foot in the down position.

▼ On the sewing machine, mark the cut edge of the paper template with several layers of masking tape or with a permanent marking pen. This mark indicates the ¼" seam allowance the template uses.

▼ If the presser foot extends beyond the cut edge of the paper template, mark the presser foot itself with the marker pen. Sometimes, special presser feet are available that have an engraved mark ¼" from the needle position.

2. Once you have marked the ¼" on your machine, trace the solid line of the pattern directly from the book onto the template cardboard or plastic.

3. Cut the template along this solid line.

4. Open your fabric so that it is a single layer and place it face down. Put the template on top of the wrong side of the fabric and trace around the template. The traced shapes can be next to one another because they already include the seam allowance. You will use your machine to keep your seam allowances even.

Marking and Cutting Cloth

CUTTING ON THE GRAINLINE

The majority of the time, I cut my fabric with the grainline, which runs in the same direction as the selvage edges (i.e., on the lengthwise grain). When cutting many pieces from one piece of fabric, this is the most economical method. This method works beautifully with solids, plaids, large flowery prints, or any fabric that is an overall design. As quilters, we like guidelines. These guidelines, such as cutting fabrics on the grain, make our lives easier when stitching fabric pieces together. However, keep in mind that there really are no hard and fast rules in quilting. Directional fabrics such as stripes and plaids almost look better if you cut them helter skelter, or off grain. This means making a point of not placing the template on either the lengthwise or crosswise grains, but placing it instead on the bias or any off-grain angle. For many quilts, cutting stripes and plaids on the bias or off grain aesthetically incorporates the fabric into the quilt as a whole rather than making a rigid vertical or diagonal statement. New quilters should be aware that pieces cut in this random manner are a little more challenging to work with. You will have three bias edges

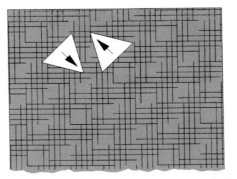

Figure 3-1 Pieces cut with the grainline

Figure 3-2 Pieces cut helter skelter, or "off grain"

on the triangles rather than two. Experienced quilters should not have any problem with this technique.

I use several methods to mark and cut. One is described in "Making Templates with No Seam Allowances" earlier in this chapter. Three more are discussed here. The first method takes advantage of the 60° triangle's shape. The other techniques involve cutting a template from paper and using Clover pins (a brand of straight pins with flat flower-heads) to hold the paper template in place.

CUTTING CLOTH USING TRIANGLE TEMPLATES WITH SEAM ALLOWANCES

One advantage of having seam allowances built into your templates is this easy marking method, which keeps the triangles on the grain.

1. Fold the fabric with right sides together so that the selvage edges are even.

2. Place the template near the selvage edge and trace around it.

3. Reposition the template so that it's abutting the shape just traced, and trace the remaining two edges.

4. Repeat Step 3 until you get close to the fold.

5. If there's room, you can place a half triangle on the fold to get another full template shape when the fabric is unfolded. Also, if the pattern requires any half triangles, these can be placed near the selvage edge as shown in Figure 3-3.

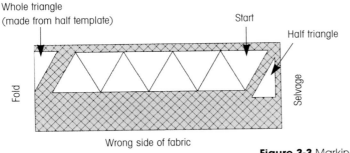

Figure 3-3 Marking cloth using a 60° triangle template with seam allowance

CUTTING LAYERED CLOTH USING TEMPLATES WITH NO SEAM ALLOWANCES

This method is for the more experienced quilter who has had some practice with a rotary cutter.

1. Layer several pieces of fabric, right side up.

2. Position the paper template on top of the fabric and pin through the template and all layers of fabric with one or more flower-head pins.

3. Use an Omni-Grid ruler (a brand of yellow-marked rulers made to be used with rotary cutters) and a rotary cutter to add a ¼" seam allowance. (There are other brands of rulers, but I like the Omni-Grid because you can easily see the fabric through it.)

CUTTING LAYERED CLOTH USING TEMPLATES WITH SEAM ALLOWANCES

1. Layer several fabrics, right side down.

2. Trace around the template as described in "Cutting Cloth Using Triangle Templates with Seam Allowances" earlier in this chapter.

3. Pin through all layers of fabric with Clover or other flower-head pins.

4. Cut using either a sharp pair of scissors or a rotary cutter.

If you are new to the rotary cutter, practice using just two to three layers of fabric. I use no more than four. I also alternate by sometimes cutting with scissors and sometimes with the rotary cutter, since I have tendinitis in my elbow.

Piecing

With the exception of *Pond Lilies,* all of the quilts in this book can be assembled by rows. Most of the rows consist of triangles and, in some cases, those triangles are themselves pieced. Generally, once individual triangles are pieced, the quilts can be assembled in rows, but I will explain the exact piecing sequence for each quilt. I will use the word *sets* to describe a pattern piece, such as a triangle, that is pieced from two or more fabric shapes. (See page 24 for a discussion of half sets and reverse half sets.)

ASSEMBLING ROWS

1. For the first row and for all odd numbered rows, finger press the seams to the left.

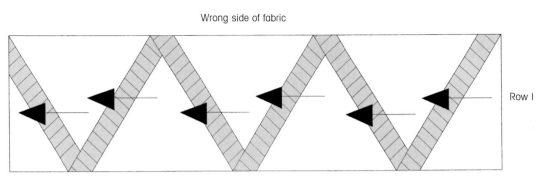

Wrong side of fabric

Row I

Figure 3-4 First row of quilt with seams finger pressed to the left

2. On the second and all even numbered rows, finger press the seams to the right.

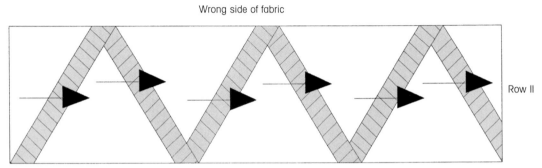

Wrong side of fabric

Row II

Figure 3-5 Second row of quilt with seams finger pressed to the right

3. Stitch the rows together, finger pressing the seams as you go.

4. After stitching the rows together, iron the seams in each row in the direction of the finger press: seams to the left on odd rows and to the right on even rows. The seams in each row will abut, making it easier to match points.

STITCHING SEQUENCE

In each chapter, directions will be given to assemble the triangles with as much straight sewing as possible. In some cases, I will show you a pivot technique that creates inset seams with a single unbroken line of machine stitching. This takes some practice, but it is well worth the effort to be able to master this little technique. Once each triangle is stitched together and ironed, just forget about the seams in it and treat it as if it were a solid piece of fabric.

Borders

Many of the quilts in this book have built-in borders between the pieced quilt and the binding. Most often these borders are mitered. A mitered border is one in which the corners meet on a diagonal seam. Instructions for mitering borders are given in the directions for the given quilt. Some of my quilts feature a special "double border." It is first shown in Chapter 7, in *Pond Lilies*. The first border is a narrow one that I call a highlighter. This type of border calls a halt to the patchwork. It separates the patchwork from the rest of the border, whether the border is plain or pieced. Sometimes I use a highlighter to call attention to the shape of the quilt, especially if it is a triangle or a hexagon. Mostly I use it because it looks good. Because this border is so narrow, I like to cut it the same length as the border next to it. Then I stitch the two border pieces together and cut them to the final length.

Most borders are cut on grain, but many times I have only ¼ yard of fabric that is just perfect for my highlighter. If my quilt dimensions are larger than 45", I then cut crossgrain strips and stitch sections together to piece the final length. When using prints, these seam lines are hardly noticeable in such a narrow band of fabric. I will give border fabric requirements for cutting the highlighter borders both on grain and across the grain.

The border lengths given in this book have been calculated by a grid. If your piecing is done by marking without seam allowances and stitching on a line, you will probably come out with the same dimensions that I do. I find that when I stitch with a ¼" seam allowance included in my template, my finished size is a little bigger. So before you cut your border strips, measure your quilt.

Ironing

Because the 60° triangle has only the bottom section on grain with the two side sections on the bias, I try not to handle my fabric too much. This includes ironing. Therefore, I do not press each piece as it is assembled. Finger press seams to one side, with light fabric toward dark whenever possible. Then finger press each section and iron the completed block. Many times I will wait until the quilt is assembled before I iron it.

Quilting

Starting with Chapter 4, this book is chock full of designs to make quilts ranging from small wallhangings to king-size bed quilts. The designs start off with very simple patterns that use only triangles, then go on to designs within a triangle, to conclude with curves and patterns that feature a very contemporary look—a little something for everyone and for every level of difficulty from simple to challenging.

All the quilts are quilted, whether by hand or by machine. If you have never quilted before, you are in for a real treat. This has always been one of my favorite parts of the process. Do not be intimidated by quilting. It is only a running stitch that holds the quilt top, the batting and the backing together. All you need is a thimble, a short needle, thread, and perhaps a little guidance from your quilt shop teacher, quilt guild friend, or a book or video. Just plunge ahead and quilt.

Experiment with short needle sizes until you find a needle length you like. Some people like #7, #8, or #9 quilting needles and others prefer a little longer sewing needle. In terms of thread, I like to use just regular thread for quilting, the same as I use when piecing. Many people like thread specifically made for quilting. This is a matter of personal preference and you will have to try both to see which you like best.

BACKING THE QUILT

Finish piecing the quilt top, then cut a backing 4" longer and 4" wider than the finished top. Cut a batting the same size as the backing. In some cases, you may have to join batts together to make the required length and width. Spread the backing over a flat surface, either a table top or the floor, with the right side of the fabric facing down. Then spread the batting over the backing fabric and finally put your pieced top, right side facing up, on top of the batting. Make sure you don't have any wrinkles in your backing or batting. It is always nice to have a friend help so that each of you can be at opposite ends, giving the backing a firm tug. If you can't get a second person, try taping the backing down with masking tape or placing books at the corners so that the backing doesn't move. When all layers are smoothly in place, baste them together with needle or thread, or pin them together with safety pins through all thicknesses at 4" intervals. Now you are almost ready to quilt.

USING A QUILTING FRAME

Lots of people use portable frames or hoops to quilt with. There are a few who don't use anything at all. I have tried oval hoops, round hoops of various sizes, and the Q-Snap plastic frames. I liked all of them at different times and for different projects. Just investigate and choose a frame that most appeals to you. Unless you have lots of room, I wouldn't recommend a large standing frame. While these are wonderful, they take up about the same amount of space as a couch and need to be left up during your quilting time. That could be several months, depending on how much time you devote to quilting. I like to spend a portion of each day working on quilting. If you do this, perhaps one-half to one hour daily, you will finish your project in no time.

TAKING YOUR FIRST QUILTING STITCHES

To begin quilting, make a very small knot in the thread. Take a stitch and hide the knot in your seam line. Use a thimble on your middle finger, and start to quilt by pushing your needle down through the fabric with your middle finger. Pick up two or three stitches on the needle, making sure you have gone through all the layers of quilt, batting, and backing. Pull the needle through the fabric and pull the thread taut. It is just like basting, only with really small stitches. That's all there is to it. Now keep on going. Every stitch you put in is one more toward your goal—a finished quilt. When you are coming toward the end of your thread, push your needle just under the first layer of fabric, in between the batting and the top, until you come out at a seam. In the seam, take three tiny stitches in the same place. Cut off the remaining thread.

Always start the quilting in the middle of the quilt when working on a portable frame. Finish each section the same day so that you don't leave the quilt stretched over the frame for long periods of time. After quilting the center section, work out toward the edges. By working from the center out, you will be keeping the backing smooth.

Remember that the point of quilting is to keep all the layers together. It is nice to have short, even stitches, but this will come in time. Just plunge in and keep on quilting; don't worry too much about the length of your stitches. I find that by picking up at least two or three stitches at a time, I can keep them pretty even. That is what you want to strive for—having your stitches and the spaces in between the same length.

Your thread length will depend on you. I like fairly long threads only because I hate to keep re-threading the needle, but most people use threads about 18" long because they don't like the thread to fray.

QUILTING INSTRUCTIONS IN THIS BOOK

Some of the quilts in this book are machine quilted—nothing fancy, mostly just in the ditch. "In the ditch" means sewing in the seam lines. I recommend a walking foot (sometimes called an even-feed foot) for machine quilting, and a few lessons at your local shop.

At the end of each project, I will tell you what type of quilting I have used. As this is just my personal choice, please feel free to change the quilting style to whatever you like. This book is about piecing quilt designs and encouraging you to explore the 60° triangle and its variations. The quilting stitch and its designs are a book unto itself. Just have fun and experiment.

Binding the Quilt

Binding is the process of covering the raw edges of the quilt—where batting, backing, and quilt top are all exposed—with fabric strips.

CREATING THE BINDING

Measure all sides of the quilt and add 5" to get the overall length of fabric needed for binding. Cut in strips that are $2\frac{1}{2}$" wide. Cut as many crossgrain strips as you need to cover the length of all the edges of the quilt (don't forget to add seam allowances if you are piecing the strip together).

Machine stitch the strips along the $2^{1}\!/_{2}"$ edges to make one long piece of fabric. Iron the seams open. With wrong sides of fabric together, fold along the long edge of the fabric strip (making the width of the fabric now $1^{1}\!/_{4}"$) and press the fold.

Attaching the Binding

Fold in one short end of the fabric 1". About 10" from a corner of the quilt, pin the folded short end of the binding to the right side of the quilt, making sure the raw edges of the binding and the quilt are even (i.e., the fold of the binding will be away from the edge). Pin the binding strip along all the edges of the quilt.

On my Pfaff machine I have a built-in walking foot that I use when stitching binding. I would recommend purchasing a walking foot if you don't have one. They can be extremely useful when stitching over bulky fabrics (such as binding) or bulking seams. A walking foot has feed dogs like the ones that are under your sewing foot. With feed dogs over the top of your fabric and under the bottom of your layers, all the bulk will move through the machine evenly, preventing puckering.

Attach the binding to the quilt by stitching $^{1}\!/_{4}"$ in from the raw edges using a stitch that is looser than the one you use to piece, but not as long or loose as a basting stitch. Stitch to within $^{1}\!/_{4}"$ of the first corner and stop. Remove the quilt from the sewing machine. On the binding, measure $^{1}\!/_{2}"$ past the stitching and put a pencil mark along the raw edge. This $^{1}\!/_{2}"$ of binding is not stitched now, but will be used to make a tuck when you hand-hem the binding to the back of the quilt. Along the next edge of the quilt, put a pencil mark $^{1}\!/_{4}"$ from the corner. Pin the pencil mark on the binding to the pencil mark on the quilt. Pin the binding all along the second edge, stopping $^{1}\!/_{4}"$ from the corner. Stitch the binding to the quilt. Repeat this process for the remaining edges. On the last edge, finish by stitching about $1^{1}\!/_{2}"$ of binding over the folded binding that you first pinned to the quilt. Be sure to fold under this last end of the binding before stitching it to the quilt.

Remove the quilt from the sewing machine and check the back of it to see if the backing is smooth. If you have any puckers, clip out several inches of stitches before and after the puckers and restitch. When the backing is smooth, trim any excess backing and batting to within $\frac{1}{4}$" of the stitching. Fold the binding to the back of the quilt so that the pressed fold sits atop the raw edge of the quilt. Hem the binding to the quilt along the stitched line. When you reach each corner, just push $\frac{1}{4}$" of the excess fabric in on the front, turn the binding, and push $\frac{1}{4}$" of fabric in on the back, making a nice little mitered edge. Sometimes I hem along the mitered edge in front and back. Hem all along the edge of the binding.

Basic Triangle Quilts

A Quilted Triptych

Nothing is more striking than the plain simplicity of triangles made of some gorgeous fabrics. Here is a set of triptychs that I made for our hall when we moved to Maine. They are this shape because they follow the lines of the stairway walls. You can make these slanted shapes (which I call "triptychs") or you can make rectangular wall quilts (which I call "wallhangings") using the converted yardage in the various cutting charts. These are great quilts to help you get started making triangle projects. Note that the wallhanging in Figure 4-2 (p. 23) can be rotated 90° to make the triangles point up and down, as in Figure 4-3 (p. 23). Sometimes a fabric has a one-way design that looks best in a particular orientation, or perhaps you might just like the looks of one design better than the other.

The wallhangings use full 60° triangles as well as half triangles. The half triangles are marked on the templates at the end of the chapter. To cut a reverse half triangle (the right-hand side of the triangle), simply flip the half-triangle template over (so that the printed side is face down) before cutting. Refer to the layout diagrams and the cutting charts to determine when half and reverse half triangles are used. The number of triangles given in the charts for the alternating fabrics is the total number of half triangles, unless stated otherwise. You can mix and match the alternate fabrics in any way you like.

TECHNIQUES

Straight Seam Sewing
Sewing Triangles in Rows
Using Contrasting, Coordinated, and Blended Fabrics

Triptych I and Wallhanging I

Triptych I and *Wallhanging I* are numbered "I" because they are a one-patch design. They are both simple but dramatic projects to start with. I have used drapery fabrics for both my main color and my alternate colors. (Warning: Drapery fabrics can be difficult to hand quilt; because they are heavy, they can be machine quilted easily, though.)

LAYOUT AND CUTTING

Use the layouts shown in Figures 4-1 through 4-3 for a variety of styles of triptychs and wallhangings. In those layouts, the dark triangle denotes the main fabric and the light triangle denotes the alternate fabrics. *Please note:* Template A at the end of this chapter is used in *Triptych I* and *Wallhanging I* for all fabrics. The markings below the templates indicate how to cut a half A and a reverse half A triangle. Fabrics for the alternate triangles can be contrasting, coordinated, or blended scraps (see pp. 1–3), or whatever combination pleases you.

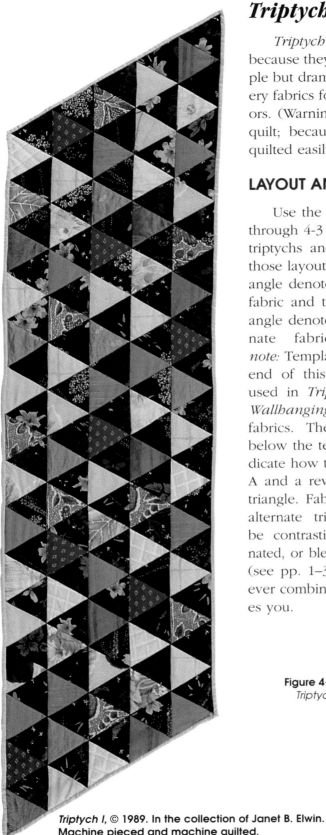

Triptych I, © 1989. In the collection of Janet B. Elwin. Machine pieced and machine quilted.

Figure 4-1 Diagram for *Triptych I,* 25½" × 90"

Figure 4-2 Diagram for *Wallhanging I*, 38¼" × 45"

Figure 4-3 Diagram for *Wallhanging I*, rotated to be 45" × 38¼"

Cutting Chart for *Triptych I* and *Wallhanging I*

	Fabric	Yardage	Template	# to Cut
Triptych I	Main fabric	1	A	90
	10 Alternate fabrics	¼ of each	A	9 of each fabric
	Binding	½		
	Backing	2⅝		
Wallhanging I	Main fabric	1	A	77
			Half A	4
			Half A reverse	4
	7 Alternate fabrics	¼ of each	A	11 of each fabric
			Half A	5
			Half A reverse	5
	Binding	⅜		
	Backing	1⅜		

STITCHING SEQUENCE

1. Lay out the triangles according to Figures 4-1, 4-2, or 4-3, incorporating the alternate fabrics in any arrangement that pleases you.

2. Stitch the rows of triangles and then join the rows.

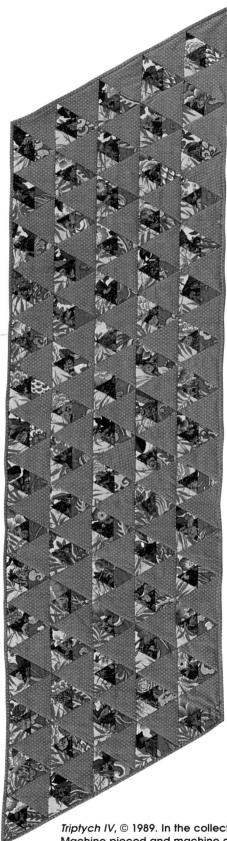

QUILTING AND BINDING

Quilt in the ditch, either by machine or by hand. For binding instructions see "Binding the Quilt" in Chapter 3.

Triptych IV and *Wallhanging IV*

Triptych IV and *Wallhanging IV* (numbered "IV" because four alternate fabrics are used) are composed of a large triangle and the four fabrics that create the alternate triangle. The wallhangings use full and half triangles made from the main fabric, and full and half sets made from the alternate fabrics. Half sets and reverse half sets are made up of half and reverse half triangles, as shown in the individual piecing illustrations (see Fig. 4-8 on p. 27, for example). When looking at the layout diagrams (Figs. 4-4, 4-5, and 4-6), keep in mind that the dark color denotes the main fabric, while the alternate triangle (the "set") is shown as four print fabrics.

Figure 4-4 Diagram for *Triptych IV,* 25½" × 90"

Triptych IV, © 1989. In the collection of Janet B. Elwin. Machine pieced and machine quilted.

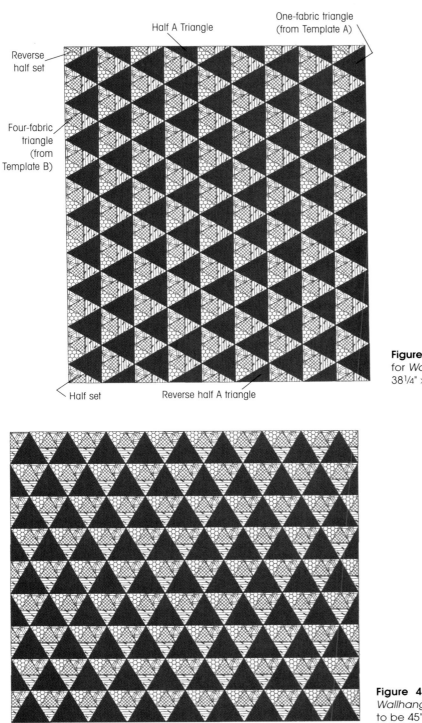

Reverse half set

Half A Triangle

One-fabric triangle (from Template A)

Four-fabric triangle (from Template B)

Half set

Reverse half A triangle

Figure 4-5 Diagram for *Wallhanging IV,* 38¼" × 45"

Figure 4-6 Diagram for *Wallhanging IV,* rotated to be 45" × 38¼"

LAYOUT AND CUTTING

Use the layouts shown in Figures 4-4 through 4-6 for the style triptych or wallhanging suitable for you. *Please note:* Template A at the end of this chapter is used for the main fabric and Template B is used for the four small triangles that create the four-fabric alternate triangle.

Cutting Chart for *Triptych IV* and *Wallhanging IV*

	Fabric	Yardage	Template	# to Cut
Triptych IV	Main fabric	1	A	90
	4 Alternate fabrics	½ of each	B	90 of each fabric
	Binding	½		
	Backing	2⅝		
Wallhanging IV	Main fabric	1	A Half A Half A reverse	77 4 4
	Alternate fabric #1	½	B Half B Half B reverse	76 5 5
	Alternate fabric #2	½	B	81
	Alternate fabric #3	½	B Half B Half B reverse	76 5 5
	Alternate fabric #4	½	B	81
	Binding	⅜		
	Backing	1⅜		

STITCHING SEQUENCE

TRIPTYCH IV

1. Assemble 90 sets of four-fabric triangles.

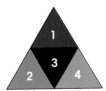

Figure 4-7 A four-fabric triangle, created using Template B

2. Lay out the one-fabric and four-fabric triangles according to Figure 4-4 on page 24.

3. Stitch in rows and join the rows.

1. Assemble 76 sets of four-fabric triangles (Fig. 4-7).

2. Assemble five half sets, as shown.

Figure 4-8 A half set of a four-fabric triangle, created using Template B

3. Assemble five reverse half sets, as shown.

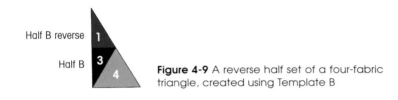

Figure 4-9 A reverse half set of a four-fabric triangle, created using Template B

4. Lay out according to Figure 4-5 or 4-6 on page 25.

5. Stitch in rows and join the rows.

QUILTING AND BINDING

Quilt in the ditch, either by machine or by hand. For binding instructions, see "Binding the Quilt" in Chapter 3.

Triptych XVI and Wallhanging XVI

Triptych XVI and *Wallhanging XVI* (numbered "XVI" because they use 16 alternate fabrics—I bet you knew that!) are composed of one large triangle and one alternate triangle made of 16 fabrics. Again, keep in mind that the dark triangle in Figures 4-10 through 4-12 denotes the main fabric; the light triangle is pieced from the 16 alternate fabrics.

LAYOUT AND CUTTING

Please note: Template A at the end of this chapter is used for the main fabric and Template C is used for the 16 small triangles that create the 16-fabric alternate triangle.

Figure 4-10 Diagram for *Triptych XVI*, 25½" × 90"

Figure 4-11 Diagram for *Wallhanging XVI*, 38¼" × 45"

Figure 4-12 Diagram for *Wallhanging XVI*, rotated to be 45" × 38¼"

	Fabric	Yardage	Template	# to Cut
Triptych XVI	Main fabric	1	A	90
	16 Alternate fabrics	¼ of each	C	90 of each fabric
	Binding	½		
	Backing	2⅝		
Wallhanging XVI	Main fabric	1	A	77
			Half A	4
			Half A reverse	4
	Alternate fabric #1	¼	C	76
			Half C	5
			Half C reverse	5
	Alternate fabric #2	¼	C	81
	Alternate fabric #3	¼	C	76
			Half C	5
			Half C reverse	5
	Alternate fabric #4	¼	C	81
	Alternate fabric #5	¼	C	76
			Half C	5
			Half C reverse	5
	Alternate fabric #6	¼	C	81
	Alternate fabric #7	¼	C	76
			Half C	5
			Half C reverse	5
	Alternate fabric #8	¼	C	81
	Alternate fabric #9	¼	C	76
			Half C	5
			Half C reverse	5
	Alternate fabric #10	¼	C	81
	Alternate fabric #11	¼	C	76
			Half C	5
			Half C reverse	5
	Alternate fabric #12	¼	C	81
	Alternate fabric #13	¼	C	76
			Half C	5
			Half C reverse	5
	Alternate fabric #14	¼	C	81
	Alternate fabric #15	¼	C	76
			Half C	5
			Half C reverse	5
	Alternate fabric #16	¼	C	81
	Binding	⅜		
	Backing	1⅜		

STITCHING SEQUENCE

TRIPTYCH XVI

1. Assemble 90 sets of the 16-fabric triangles shown.

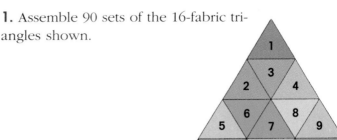

Figure 4-13 A 16-fabric triangle, created using Template C

2. Lay out the one-fabric and 16-fabric triangles according to Figure 4-10 (p.28).

3. Stitch in rows and join the rows.

WALLHANGING XVI

1. Assemble 76 sets of 16-fabric triangles.

2. Assemble five half sets, using half C triangles and half C reverse triangles as shown.

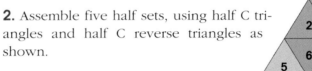

Figure 4-14 A half set of a 16-fabric triangle, created using Template C

3. Assemble five reverse half sets, using half C reverse and half C triangles as shown in Figure 4-15.

4. Lay out the one-fabric and 16-fabric triangles according to Figure 4-11 or 4-12 (p.28).

5. Stitch in rows and join the rows.

Figure 4-15 A reverse half set of a 16-fabric triangle, created using Template C

QUILTING AND BINDING

Quilt in the ditch, either by machine or by hand. To bind, see "Binding the Quilt" in Chapter 3.

Triptych XVI, © 1989. In the collection of Janet B. Elwin. Machine pieced and machine quilted.

Variations on a Theme: Full-Size Quilts

Once you start cutting and piecing triangles, it's like popcorn. You want to make more. Here are some full-size quilts.

Basic Triangle Quilt

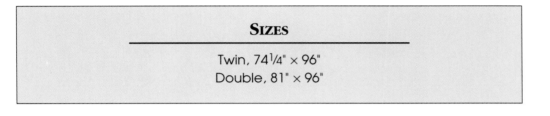

SIZES
Twin, 74¼" × 96"
Double, 81" × 96"

LAYOUT AND CUTTING

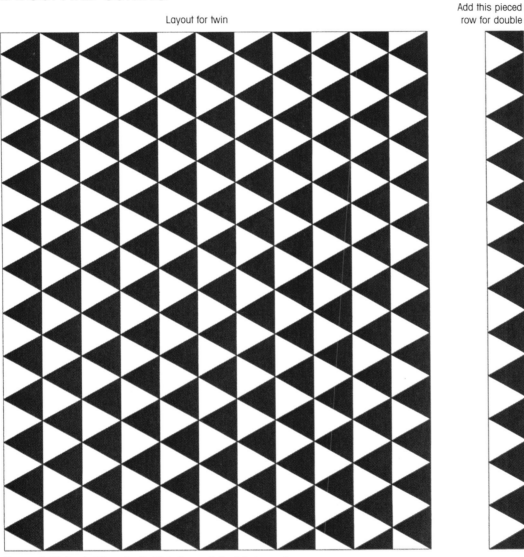

Layout for twin

Add this pieced row for double

Figure 4-16 *Basic Triangle Quilt*, twin and double layout

Cutting Chart for *Basic Triangle Quilt*

	Fabric	Yardage	Template	# to Cut
Twin	Main fabric	4½	D Half D Half D reverse	127 5 5
	6 Alternate fabrics	1 of each	D Half D Half D reverse	21 of each fabric 1 of each fabric 1 of each fabric
	Binding	⅝		
	Backing	5¼		
Double	Main fabric	5	D Half D Half D reverse	138 6 6
	6 Alternate fabrics	1 of each	D Half D Half D reverse	23 of each fabric 1 of each fabric 1 of each fabric
	Binding	⅝		
	Backing	5¼		

STITCHING SEQUENCE

1. Lay out the quilt as shown in Figure 4-16 on page 31.

2. Stitch in rows and join the rows.

QUILTING AND BINDING

Quilt in the ditch, either by machine or by hand. For binding instructions, see "Binding the Quilt" in Chapter 3.

Medallion Quilt, Queen

SIZE
98" × 96"

LAYOUT AND CUTTING

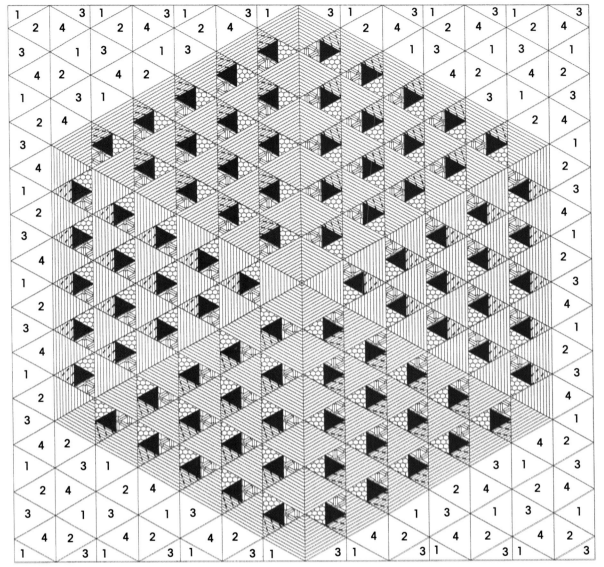

Figure 4-17 *Medallion Quilt,* queen layout

FABRIC KEY

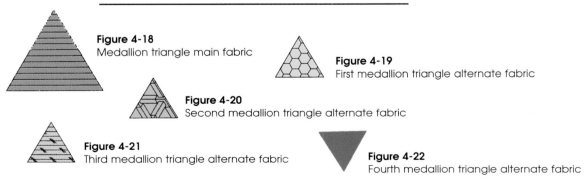

Figure 4-18
Medallion triangle main fabric

Figure 4-19
First medallion triangle alternate fabric

Figure 4-20
Second medallion triangle alternate fabric

Figure 4-21
Third medallion triangle alternate fabric

Figure 4-22
Fourth medallion triangle alternate fabric

The layout for this queen-size quilt is similar to the traditional Medallion-style design, but it utilizes triangles. This could be made with calicoes or beautiful cotton prints. Or, to create a very sophisticated quilt, use drapery fabrics. Drapery fabrics are sturdy, sew and wear well, plus they have some grand designs. The only drawback is that they are difficult to hand quilt. Trust me, I have done just that and it led to tendinitis. Drapery fabrics can be machine quilted very easily.

Cutting Chart for *Medallion Quilt*

	Fabric	Yardage	Template	# to Cut
Medallion in Queen and King Size*				
	Main fabric	4	D	126
	4 Alternate fabrics	7/8 of each	E	90 of each fabric
Background**	Background color #1	1 1/8	D Half D Half D reverse	23 7 7
	Background color #2	1 1/8	D	30
	Background color #3	1 1/8	D Half D Half D reverse	23 7 7
	Background color #4	1 1/8	D	30
Binding	Queen binding	5/8		
	King binding	3/4		
Backing	Queen backing	6 1/4		
	King backing	9 3/4		

* The king-size quilt has the same layout as the queen, but an additional border is added, as explained in *"Medallion Quilt*, King" later in this chapter.

** Look at the background fabrics in *Return to Dresden* in Chapter 6. I have used four blended pink fabrics. This could also be done with four blended muted prints such as white-on-white and beige-on-beige combinations.

STITCHING SEQUENCE

1. Assemble 96 sets of the alternate fabric triangles, created using Template E.

Figure 4-23 Assembled alternate fabric triangle

2. Lay out the quilt according to Figure 4-17 (p. 33) and stitch in rows. Join the rows.

Medallion Quilt, King

LAYOUT AND CUTTING

This quilt has the same layout as the queen (see Figure 4-17 on p. 33). Just add an unmitered border of an appropriate fabric.

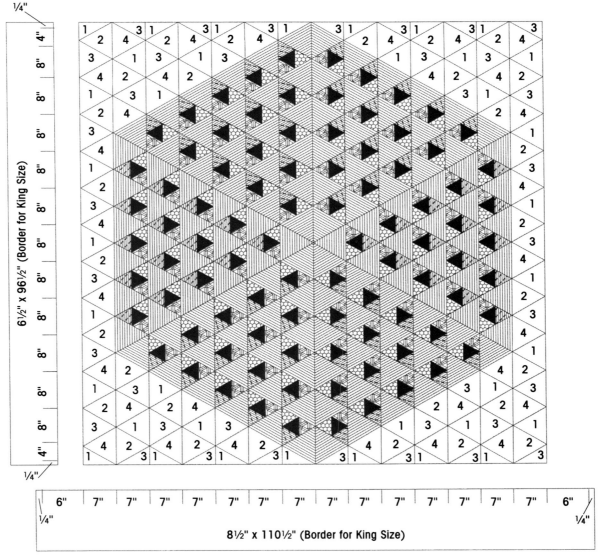

Figure 4-24 Layout for king-size *Medallion Quilt*

Cutting Chart for Border to King-Size *Medallion Quilt*

	Fabric	Yardage	Template	# to Cut
Border for King	As desired	3⅛	6½" × 96½"	2
			8½" × 110½"	2

STITCHING SEQUENCE

1. For the main body of the quilt, use the same stitching sequence as for the queen-size.

2. For the border, use the following notch technique for a perfect border: On each 6½" × 96½" strip, make a pencil mark ¼" in from the left end for seam allowance. This border will go on one of the two short sides of the quilt.

3. Moving from left to right, place the next mark 4" further, then mark every 8" eleven times. The next mark is 4" further. The last one will be ¼" from the right end. This is for seam allowance.

4. Match the notches of one border to the seams in the body of the quilt. Pin at each notch. Repeat for the opposite border.

5. Stitch the two short borders to the body of the quilt.

6. On each 8½" × 110½" strip, make a pencil mark ¼" in from the left end for the seam allowance. This border will go on one of the two long sides of the quilt.

7. Make the next mark 6" to the right of the last mark. This allows for the side border already in place.

8. Moving from left to right, place a pencil mark every 7" fourteen times. The next mark is 6" further, for the side border.

9. Mark ¼" from the right end for the seam allowance.

10. Match the notches of one border to the seams in the body of the quilt. Pin at each notch. Repeat for the opposite border.

11. Stitch the two long borders to the quilt.

QUILTING AND BINDING

Quilt in the ditch, either by machine or by hand. For binding instructions, see "Binding the Quilt" in Chapter 3.

Vertical Triangle Quilt

Here are several more layouts for bed-size quilts. If you refer back to the twin and double bed layouts in Figure 4-16 (p. 31), you'll notice the sideways position of the triangle. The orientation of the triangle for the queen and king *Medallion Quilt* was the same. The triangles in the following layouts, however, have their points going down, not to the side. This will change the sizes of the quilts a little, so don't think these measurements are incorrect. If you choose a one-way fabric, you will need to be aware of the orientation of the different triangles in order to keep the print going in the same direction on all triangles.

LAYOUT AND CUTTING

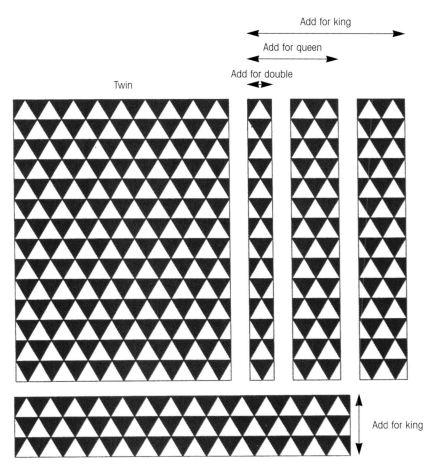

Figure 4-25 Layout for twin-, double-, queen-, and king-size *Vertical Triangle Quilt*

Yardage for each size quilt will be calculated for use in two ways. The first table (p. 38) shows the yardage using a main fabric and one other fabric. The second table (pp. 39–40) is for a main fabric and four fabrics in each alternate triangle. Alternate triangles are shown as white in Figure 4-25.

Cutting Chart for *Vertical Triangle Quilt with One Alternate Fabric*

	Fabric	Yardage	Template	# to Cut
Twin (72" x 98")	Main fabric	4¼	D Half D Half D reverse	119 7 7
	Alternate fabric	4¼	D Half D Half D reverse	119 7 7
	Binding	⅝		
	Backing	5¼		
Double (80" x 94½")	Main fabric	4¾	D Half D Half D reverse	133 7 7
	Alternate fabric	4¾	D Half D Half D reverse	133 7 7
	Binding	⅝		
	Backing	5¼		
Queen (96" x 100½")	Main fabric	5½	D Half D Half D reverse	161 7 7
	Alternate fabric	5½	D Half D Half D reverse	161 7 7
	Binding	⅝		
	Backing	6¼		
King (112" x 114½")	Main fabric	7½	D Half D Half D reverse	229 9 9
	Alternate fabric	7½	D Half D Half D reverse	230 8 8
	Binding	¾		
	Backing	9¾		

Cutting Chart for *Vertical Triangle Quilt with Four Alternate Fabrics*

	Fabric	Yardage	Template	# to Cut
Twin (72" x 98")	Main fabric	4¼	D Half D Half D reverse	119 7 7
	Alternate fabric #1	1⅛	E Half E Half E reverse	119 7 7
	Alternate fabric #2	1⅛	E	126
	Alternate fabric #3	1⅛	E Half E Half E reverse	119 7 7
	Alternate fabric #4	1⅛	E	126
	Binding	⅝		
	Backing	5¼		
Double (80" x 94½")	Main fabric	4¾	D Half D Half D reverse	133 7 7
	Alternate fabric #1	1¼	E Half E Half E reverse	133 7 7
	Alternate fabric #2	1¼	E	141
	Alternate fabric #3	1¼	E Half E Half E reverse	133 7 7
	Alternate fabric #4	1¼	E	141
	Binding	⅝		
	Backing	5¼		
Queen (96" x 100½")	Main fabric	5½	D Half D Half D reverse	161 7 7
	Alternate fabric #1	1½	E Half E Half E reverse	161 7 7
	Alternate fabric #2	1½	E	168
	Alternate fabric #3	1½	E Half E Half E reverse	161 7 7
	Alternate fabric #4	1½	E	168

Cutting Chart for *Vertical Triangle Quilt with Four Alternate Fabrics* (continued)

	Fabric	Yardage	Template	# to Cut
Queen (cont.)	Binding	⅝		
	Backing	6¼		
King **(112" x 114½")**	Main fabric	7½	D Half D Half D reverse	229 9 9
	Alternate fabric #1	1⅞	E Half E Half E reverse	222 8 8
	Alternate fabric #2	1⅞	E	230
	Alternate fabric #3	1⅞	E Half E Half E reverse	222 8 8
	Alternate fabric #4	1⅞	E	230
	Binding	¾		
	Backing	9¾		

STITCHING SEQUENCE

To make the quilt with four alternate fabrics, refer to Figures 4-7 through 4-9 and the assembly instructions for *Wallhanging IV* on pages 24–27. Lay out the size quilt you want according to Figure 4-25 on page 37, and stitch in rows. Then join the rows. Add borders if desired.

QUILTING AND BINDING

Quilt in the ditch, either by machine or by hand. For binding instructions, see "Binding the Quilt" in Chapter 3.

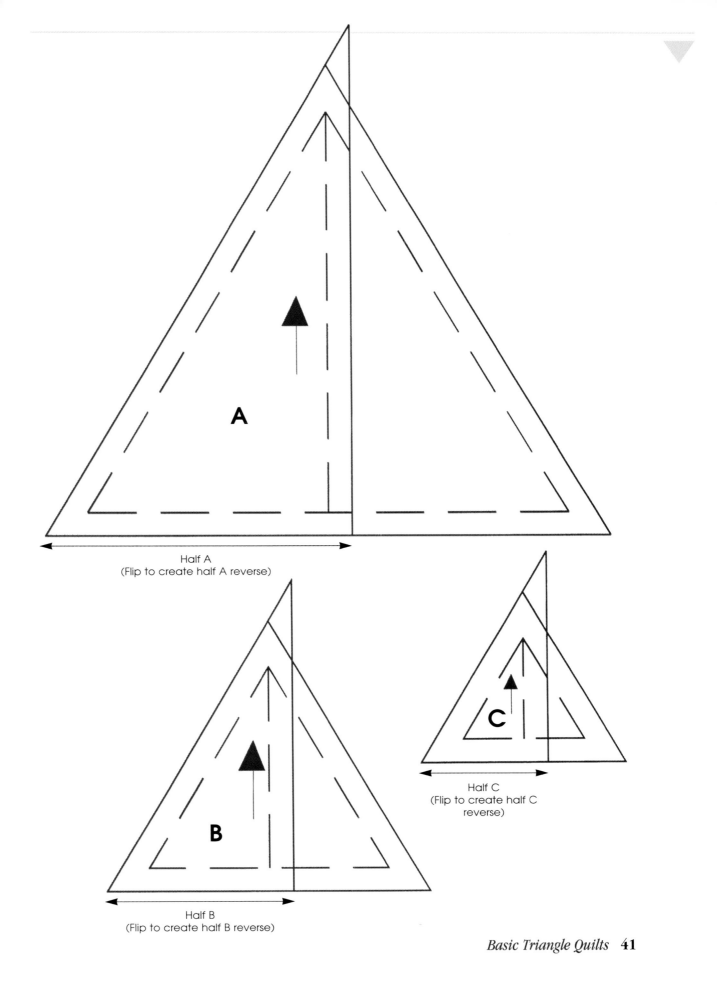

Half A
(Flip to create half A reverse)

Half B
(Flip to create half B reverse)

Half C
(Flip to create half C
reverse)

A

B

C

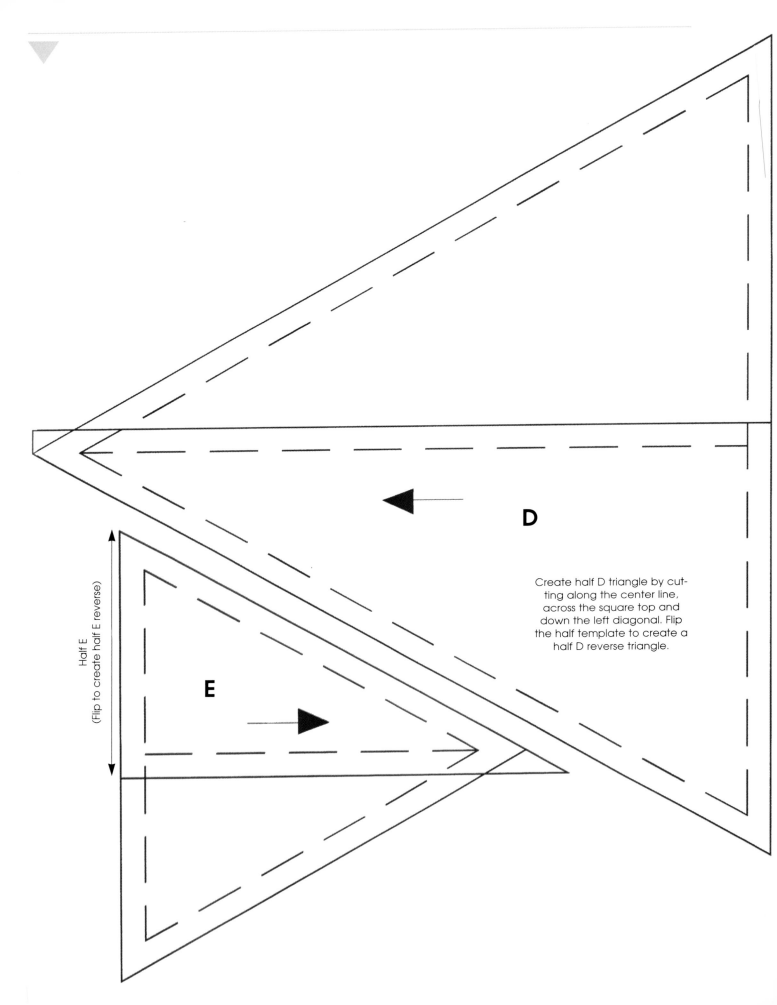

D

Create half D triangle by cutting along the center line, across the square top and down the left diagonal. Flip the half template to create a half D reverse triangle.

E

Half E
(Flip to create half E reverse)

Contemporary Quilts

A Year in the Life of My Tree

TECHNIQUES

Straight Seam Sewing
Using Contrasting, Coordinated, and Blended Fabrics
Piecing a Border

This quilt was made to celebrate a beautiful maple tree next to our house when we lived in Massachusetts. The tree was tall and full, and each season brought a different beauty to it. Our land in Maine is filled with beautiful fir, birch, and oak trees that I love—especially the fir, which keeps its green needles all year long and gives a lot of color to our otherwise dreary long gray days of winter. But I do miss looking out my window at that lovely Massachusetts maple tree, especially in autumn.

LAYOUT AND CUTTING

The pattern for "My Tree" is an adaptation of several square designs that are familiar to most quilters. It is fairly simple—just rows of triangles. I made eight trees: one for each of the four seasons and one for each season in between. Each tree is highlighted by large triangles that form a star when you squint your eyes. I had a difficult time deciding on an overall background for this quilt. I tried sky blue and the trees looked as if they were floating. I tried earth brown and they looked dead. A quilting friend, Sue Turbak, suggested I change the background colors as the seasons change. Well, of course, she was absolutely right and helped me to organize this. Her suggestion saved the quilt and made the trees come to life.

A Year in the Life of My Tree, © 1986. In the collection of Janet B. Elwin. Machine pieced and hand quilted.

In working this pattern, start with the trees, then select your "star" background fabric, and then finally the backgrounds for the seasons. The sewing is simple, but the fabric selection will be your challenge. For each tree, I suggest you use two fabrics. If you have a large fabric collection, please feel free to make your trees as colorful as you like.

The leaf part of each tree will require two different fabrics. The colors I used for the trees are given in the color chart on page 46.

You will notice that the colors progress from one season to the next, except in the case of Spring (Spring green and tan) into Spring-Summer (Spring green and medium green). I purposely did not continue tan into the Spring-Summer

Figure 5-1 Diagram for *A Year in the Life of My Tree,* 54" × 63"

tree because at that time of year trees are mostly that hard-to-work-with new green and a beautiful medium green. If you are trying to recreate your favorite tree, which may be different from my beautiful Massachusetts maple leaf, please feel free to change the suggested colors for each season to more specifically represent your personal tree in your area.

Color Chart for *A Year in the Life of My Tree*

Season	Color of Tree
Summer	Medium Green and Dark Green
Summer-Fall	Dark Green and Orange
Fall	Orange and Gold
Fall-Winter	Gold and Black/White #1
Winter	Black/White #1 and Black/White #2
Winter-Spring	Black/White #2 and Spring Green
Spring	Spring Green and Tan
Spring-Summer	Spring Green and Medium Green

Cutting Chart for *A Year in the Life of My Tree*

	Fabric	Yardage	Template	# to Cut
Trees	Dark Green	1/4	A	64
	Medium Green	1/4	A	64
	Spring Green	3/8	A	96
	Orange	1/4	A	64
	Gold	1/4	A	64
	Black/White #1	1/4	A	64
	Black/White #2	1/4	A	64
	Tan	1/4	A	32
Trunk	Brown	1/4	A	16
			B	8
Trunk Background	One Summer Color	1/8	C	2
			C reverse	2
	One Fall Color	1/8	C	2
			C reverse	2
	One Winter Color	1/8	C	2
			C reverse	2
	One Spring Color	1/8	C	2
			C reverse	2
Seasons Background	Fall: Several Tans	3/4 total	D	16
			Half D	2
			Half D reverse	2

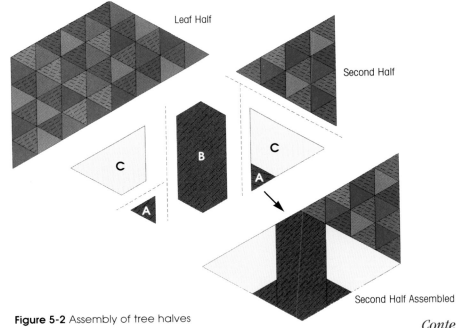

Cutting Chart for *A Year in the Life of My Tree* (cont.)

	Fabric	Yardage	Template	# to Cut
Seasons Background (cont.)	Winter: Several Whites	½ total	D Half D Half D reverse	8 2 2
	Spring: Greens and Gray/Blacks	½ total	D	13
	Summer: Golds and Blues	½ total	D Half D Half D reverse	7 2 2
Star Background	Brown	1⅛	D Half D Half D reverse	28 2 2
Binding		½		
Backing		2¾		

STITCHING SEQUENCE

1. Assemble the leaf half of each tree using two colors of A triangles or several colors, as shown in the layout in Figure 5-2.

2. Assemble the second half of each tree, which includes the rest of the leaves, the trunk (made from Templates A and B), and the two trunk background pieces.

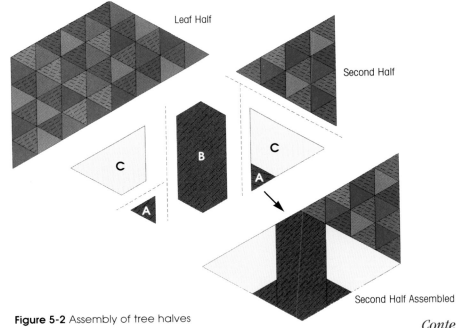

Figure 5-2 Assembly of tree halves

3. Do not stitch the two halves together yet.

4. Lay out the pieces for the entire quilt, including the seasons background pieces (marked "Spring," "Winter," etc. in Figure 5-1 on p. 45) and the star background pieces, which are the shaded triangles that surround each tree in Figure 5-1.

5. Stitch the pieces together in diagonal rows and stitch the rows together.

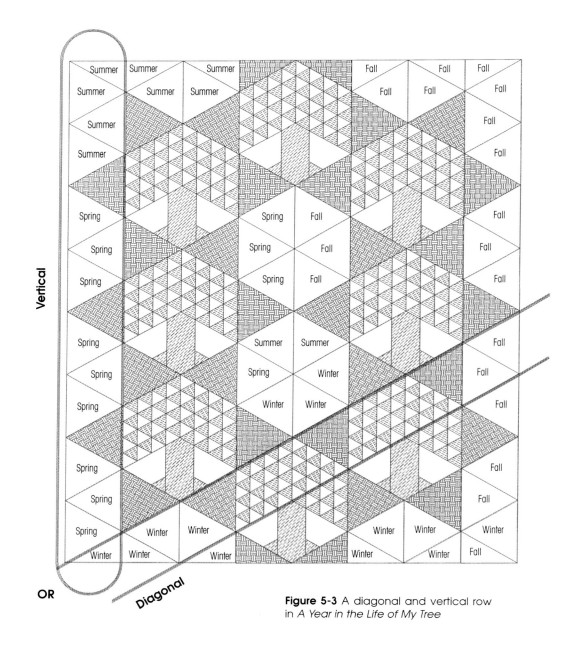

Figure 5-3 A diagonal and vertical row in *A Year in the Life of My Tree*

QUILTING AND BINDING

Quilt in the ditch by hand. For binding instructions, see "Binding the Quilt" in Chapter 3.

Lavender Blue

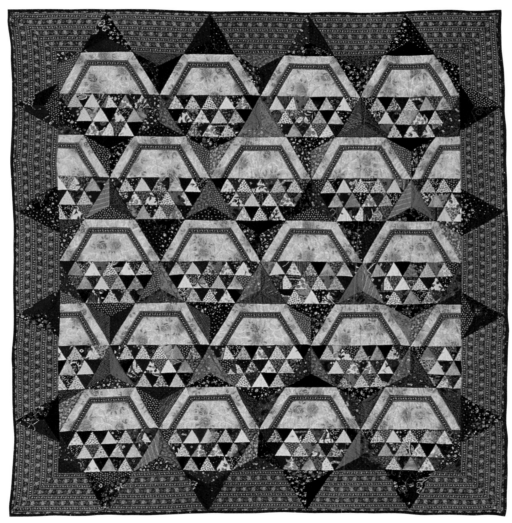

Lavender Blue, © 1986. In the collection of Janet B. Elwin. Machine pieced and hand quilted.

Baskets are an old-time favorite pattern of quilters, but there is no reason why they have to be square in shape. I redesigned this from an oldie I had seen at an auction, giving it a fresh look. Like *A Year in the Life of My Tree* quilt, these beautiful baskets are also separated by stars. But notice, these triangles are split into three sections.

This quilt was made from lots of scraps left from other purple triangle projects. I simplified the fabric requirements in the cutting chart by having you use only several fabrics. If you have a large supply of scraps, go ahead and have fun making each of the baskets different.

LAYOUT AND CUTTING

Figure 5-4 Diagram for *Lavender Blue* hexagon basket quilt, 58" × 61"

Cutting Chart for *Lavender Blue*

	Fabric	Yardage	Template	# to Cut
Basket	Medium purple	1¼	A	298
			Half A	2
			Half A reverse	2
	Light purple, pink or white	1	A	236
			Half A	4
			Half A reverse	4
Handles	Medium purple	½	G	58
			Half G	2
			Half G reverse	2
Background	Pale pink	1¼	E	18
			Half E	2
			Half E reverse	2
			F	58
			Half F	2
			Half F reverse	2
Pieced Triangles	Dark purple #1	⅝	H	60
	Dark purple #2	⅝	H	60
	Dark purple #3	⅝	H	54
			Half H	6
			Half H reverse	6
Border	Medium purple	1	I	12
			J	2
			J reverse	2
			K	2
			K reverse	2
Binding		½		
Backing		2¾		

STITCHING SEQUENCE

1. Arrange basket triangles in rows and stitch. Alternate two colors or mix and match several, as shown below.

Figure 5-5 Layout of triangles for basket

2. Stitch basket background F to basket handle G. Complete all sets.

Figure 5-6 Assembly of outer background to basket handle

3. Pin three FG sets to one basket background E, placing pins at the ¼" cross-seams as shown in Figure 5-7. Stitch from pin to pin for the center piece and from pin to edge for the left and right sections.

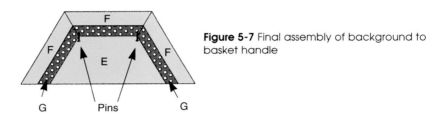

Figure 5-7 Final assembly of background to basket handle

4. Stitch the remaining seams (those between the FG sets), which will self-miter, from pin to edge. Set aside.

5. For the pieced triangles (made using Template H), pin fabric #1 to fabric #2 at the ¼" cross-seams as shown in Figure 5-8. Stitch along the short side from pin to edge.

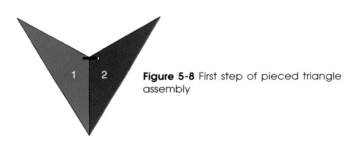

Figure 5-8 First step of pieced triangle assembly

6. There are two methods of setting in the fabric #3 triangle. The first one is a pivot method and the second is the standard set-in method.

▼ **Pivot Method:** Starting at the outside edge, stitch fabric #3 to fabric #1 along the short sides, stitching as far as the ¼" seam joining fabrics #1 and #2. Leave the needle in the down position. Lift the presser foot, pull fabric #3 around, and line it up with the remaining short side of fabric #2. Lower the presser foot. Stitch over the seam allowance to the edge of the fabric.

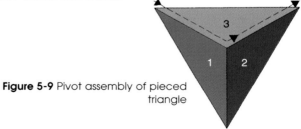

Figure 5-9 Pivot assembly of pieced triangle

▼ **Set-In Method:** Pin fabric #3 to fabric #2 of the assembled fabrics #1 and #2, placing the pin at the ¼" seam line and pushing the seam allowance away from the sewing area. Stitch from the center pin to the edge (Figure 5-10). Remove the pins. Repin fabric #3 to fabric #1, again placing the pin at the ¼" seam line and pushing the seam allowance away from the sewing area. Stitch from the center pin to the edge on the other side (Figure 5-11). Finger press seam to the left.

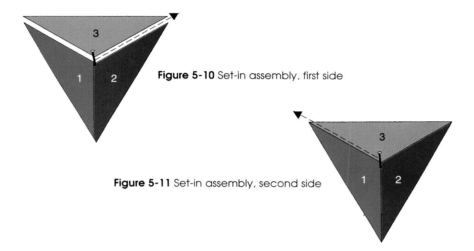

Figure 5-10 Set-in assembly, first side

Figure 5-11 Set-in assembly, second side

7. Complete half baskets and half triangle sections in the same manner described in Steps 1–6.

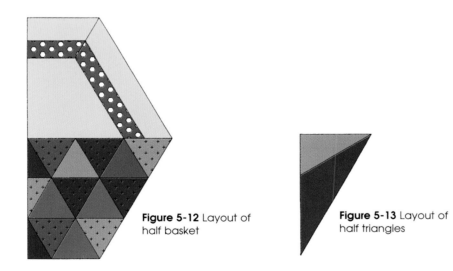

Figure 5-12 Layout of half basket

Figure 5-13 Layout of half triangles

8. Arrange all basket sections and triangles according to Figure 5-4 on page 50. Piece together as shown in Figure 5-14 on page 54.

Figure 5-14 Assembly of baskets and pieced triangles

9. Arrange the border sections (Templates I, J, K, and pieced triangles) according to Figure 5-4 on page 50. Stitch the pieces together, creating four borders (two sides, top, and bottom). Stitch to the center basket section of the quilt. Stitch the self-mitering borders.

QUILTING AND BINDING

Quilt in the ditch for baskets and stars. Freehand leaves are drawn in and quilted for basket background and border. Quilt by machine or by hand. For binding instructions, see "Binding the Quilt" in Chapter 3.

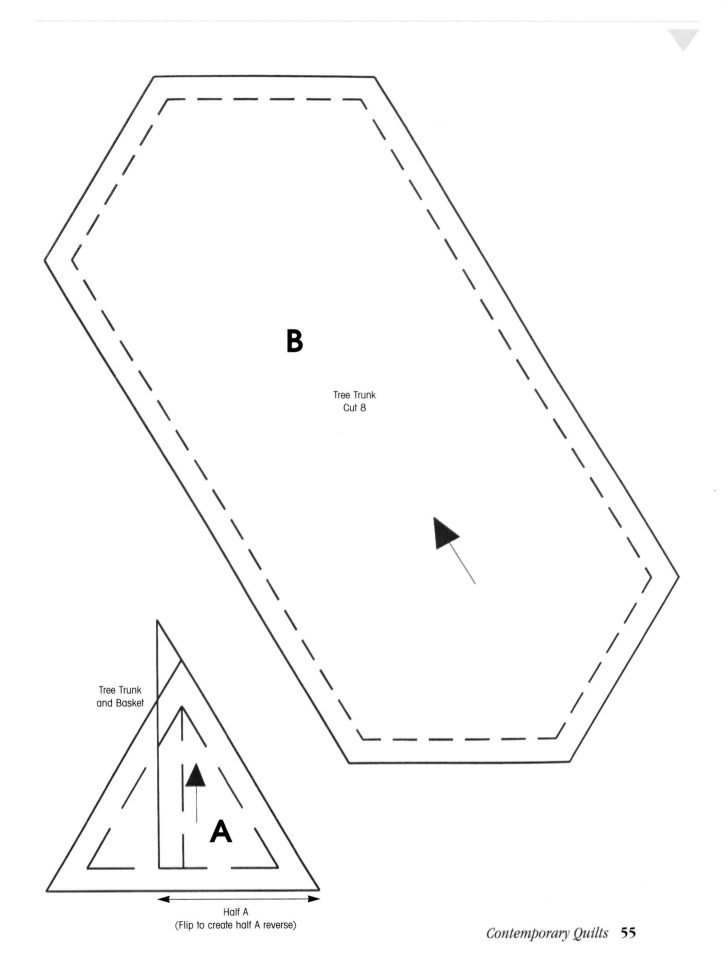

B

Tree Trunk
Cut 8

Tree Trunk
and Basket

A

Half A
(Flip to create half A reverse)

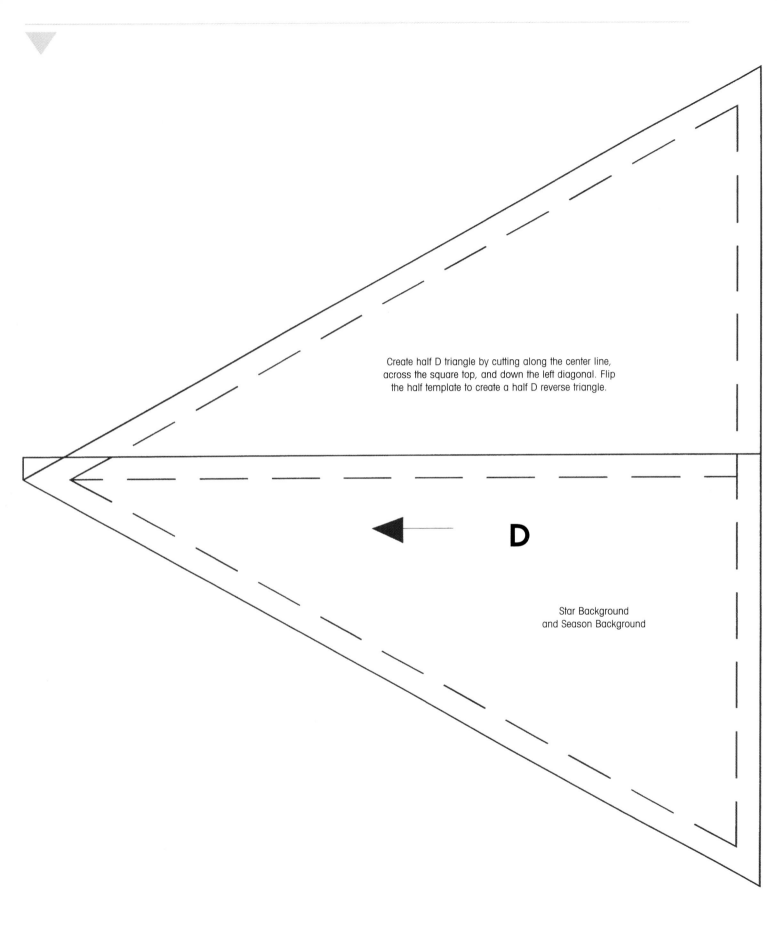

Create half D triangle by cutting along the center line,
across the square top, and down the left diagonal. Flip
the half template to create a half D reverse triangle.

D

Star Background
and Season Background

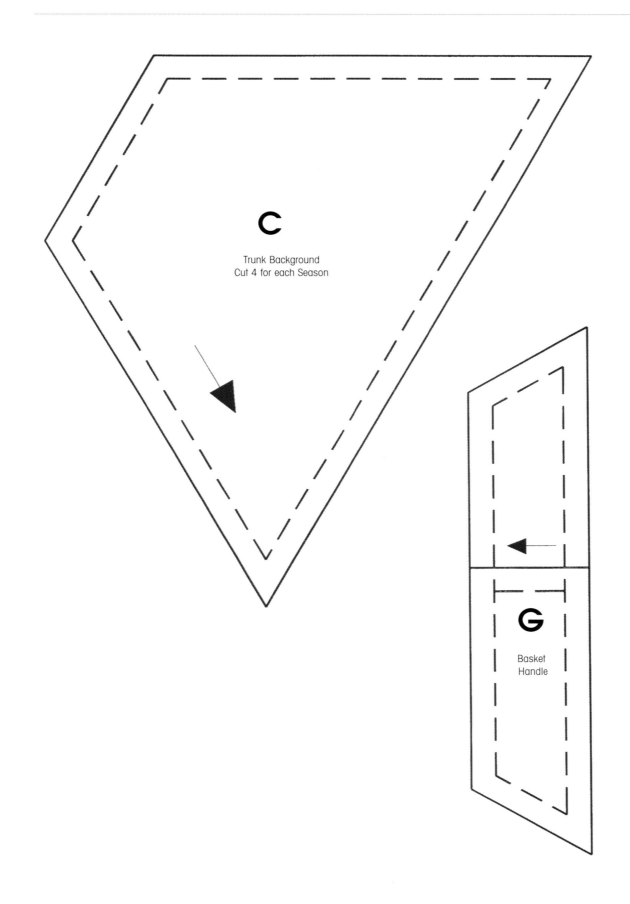

C

Trunk Background
Cut 4 for each Season

G

Basket
Handle

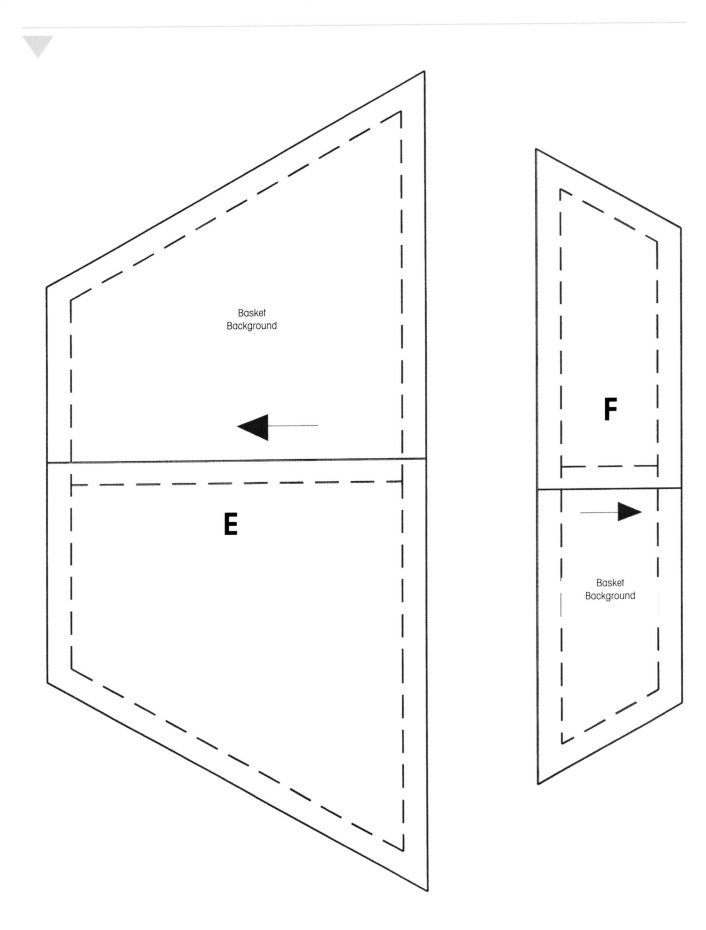

Basket
Background

E

F

Basket
Background

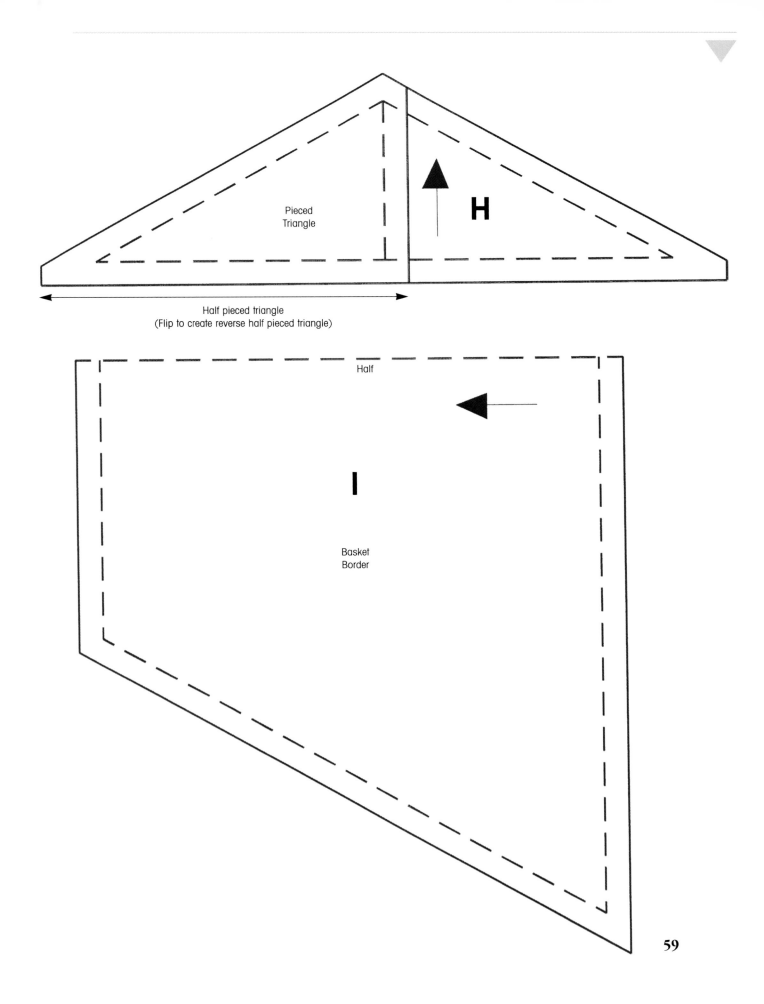

Pieced
Triangle

H

Half pieced triangle
(Flip to create reverse half pieced triangle)

Half

I

Basket
Border

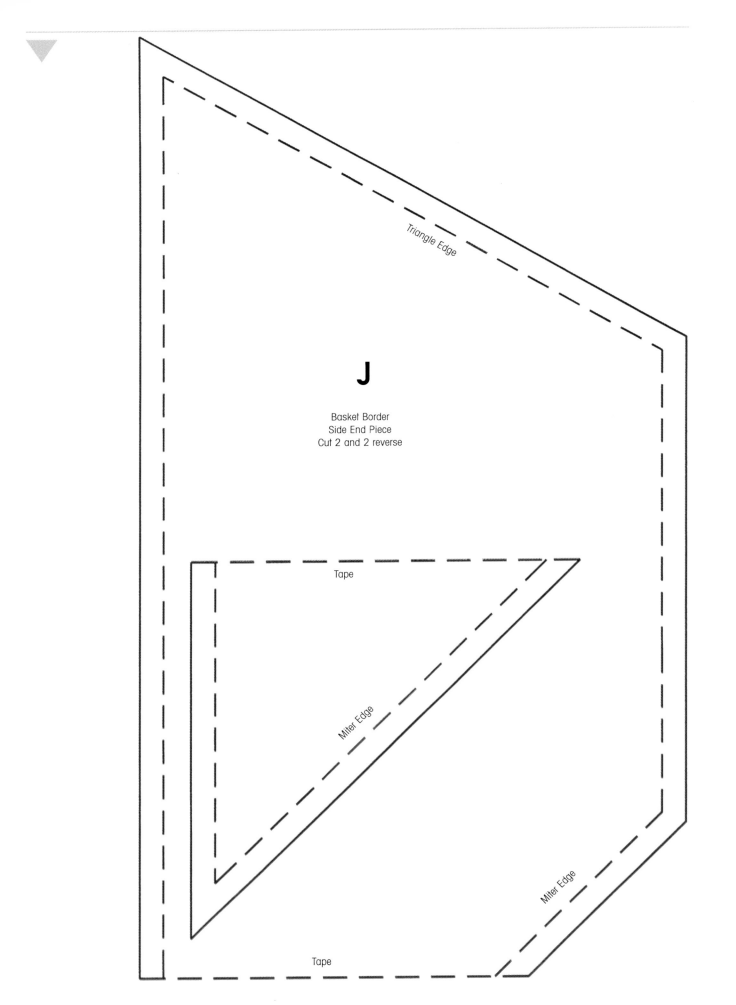

J

Basket Border
Side End Piece
Cut 2 and 2 reverse

Triangle Edge

Tape

Miter Edge

Miter Edge

Tape

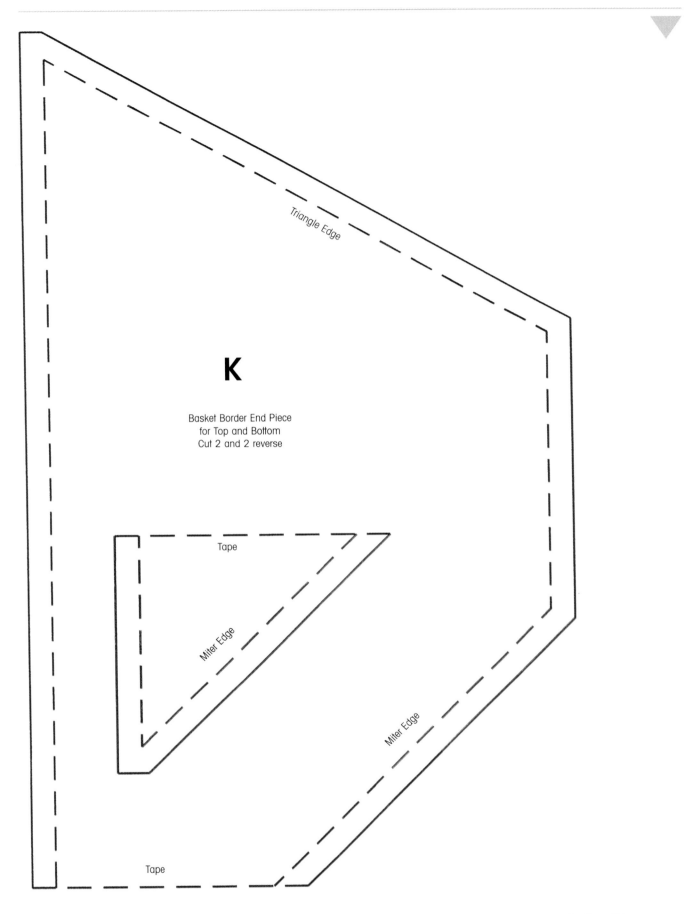

K

Basket Border End Piece
for Top and Bottom
Cut 2 and 2 reverse

Triangle Edge

Tape

Miter Edge

Miter Edge

Tape

All-Pieced Fan and Dresden Plates

The traditional Fan and Dresden Plate quilt patterns are personal favorites of mine. When I was a child, I slept under a quilt made in the '30s by my great grandmother, Sara Brown Lewis. It was golden yellow Dresden Plates sewn on a pale yellow background. I had that quilt for many years and loved tracing my fingers around the "ties" and looking at the various print fabrics. I don't remember what happened to it. I'm sure it just disintegrated from constant use. I didn't think about that quilt until many years later when my husband's grandmother, Eva Hoyt Maze, started to quilt again after her retirement. She loved Fan and Dresden Plate quilts and made many of them for relatives and also for sale. Hers were mostly "scrap" quilts (fabrics that we had great fun buying) sewn on white or muslin blocks. The recipient of the quilt would choose the color for the centers of the Fans or Dresden Plates and the lattice and/or borders. Gram was always piecing a quilt or putting in the quilting stitches at her frame. And the quilts were always lovingly received and used.

Coincidentally, the very first pattern that a group of my friends and I chose to have Gram teach us was the Fan pattern. We worked with scraps left over from other sewing projects. This was the early '70s and scraps were really scraps, but we did buy the gold background fabric. Somehow and somewhere in the process, we decided to turn it into a Dresden Plate quilt and raffle it at our church fair. This started a tradition for me with Dresden Plate quilts, and it also started a tradition at our church of a yearly quilt raffle.

I had not made a Dresden Plate quilt for many years and didn't think I would ever redesign it from its traditional square. After Gram died in 1988, I couldn't help but think of her, her love of quilts, and her sharing of those quilts and herself with our family. I missed her and our times together, and my thoughts naturally drifted to making a quilt in her memory. What resulted was a series of quilts, all of which were off-shoots of her Fan and Dresden Plate patterns. I had never done a series before and didn't start out to do so, but one quilt led to another and it was with much love and many happy memories of Gram that I made the following quilts.

When redesigning this old favorite, I could just as easily have made a Dresden Plate and then appliquéd it onto a hexagon. I did this in the bonus pattern *Necktie Quilt* included in this chapter (see page 75). But I really prefer piecing to appliquéing, and since designing is part of the little challenges and goals I set for myself, I thought a pieced background would complement the plates. When I first designed the quilt, I thought of stitching sections together into hexagons, but after studying the design, I found it was much simpler to break it down into triangles. Then, not only was the sewing straight once the triangles were made, but the design possibilities were greater. This is the first use of designs within the triangles and of triangles as a design base. The *Blue Dresden Plates* quilt is very traditional looking, except for its lovely blended background. I have only included one setting for the *Green Fans,* but I am sure you could come up with several versions of your own.

Special Techniques Used in Fan and Dresden Plate Quilts

Each triangle section of the Fans and Dresden Plates will have four background sections created by arranging Templates B and C (and their reverses) as shown on page 81, where the full-size templates are given.

1. Pin together the B and C sections and stitch from ¼" down from top right to the bottom of the fabric using a ¼" seam allowance. Finger press fabric to the left.

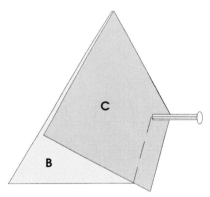

Figure 6-1 Stitching B and C sections

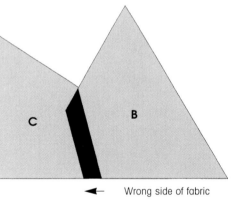

← Wrong side of fabric

Figure 6-2 Stitched sections after finger pressing

2. Pin together the C reverse and B reverse sections and stitch from ¼" down from top right to the bottom of the fabric using a ¼" seam allowance. Finger press the fabric to the left.

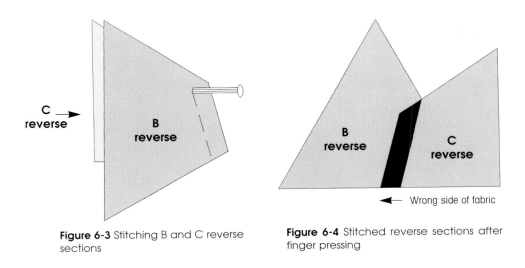

Figure 6-3 Stitching B and C reverse sections

Figure 6-4 Stitched reverse sections after finger pressing

← Wrong side of fabric

3. Insert the fan A (cut from Template A) into the BC section by either of the following two methods.

▼ **Pivot Method:** Pin fan A to piece B, right sides together with the fan on top, as shown in Figure 6-5. Stitch from the edge of the fabric to the BC seam line, leave the needle in the down position at the seam line, lift the presser foot, and pull the fan fabric around to line it up with the C fabric. Stitch over the seam allowance to the edge of the fabric.

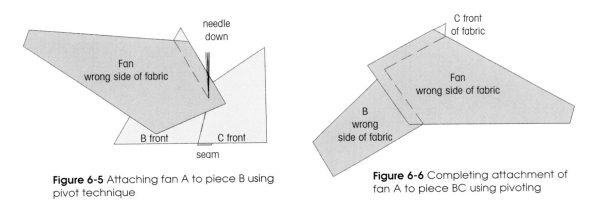

Figure 6-5 Attaching fan A to piece B using pivot technique

Figure 6-6 Completing attachment of fan A to piece BC using pivoting

▼ **Set-In Method:** This is the traditional method. Pin fan A onto piece C. Push the seam allowance away from the area to be sewn. Sew from the center seam to the edge of the fabric. Remove pins. Repin the fan to the B piece. Push the seam allowance away from the area to be sewn. Stitch from the center to the edge of the fabric. Finger press the seam to the left.

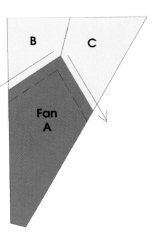

Figure 6-7 Attaching fan A to piece BC using traditional inset technique

Green Fans

I have made this and the *Blue Dresden Plates* wall hangings from scraps because I always seem to have lots of pieces left over from other projects. In coordinating my scraps, I just pile the fabrics on the floor—grouping together as many in a color range (such as the green for this quilt) as I can find in my stash. I just throw them in a pile and step away. I pull out the ones that really jar me—the ones that really don't go. Trust me, all greens (or reds or blues) won't coordinate. There are bound to be some that are too light or too dark. Find a group of fabrics that look good together and are pleasing to the eye. Cut the quantity you need and throw them into a paper bag or a shoe box. Then really mix them around as if you were mixing up raffle tickets. When you are ready to sew, just pull out the two pieces you need to make the triangle set.

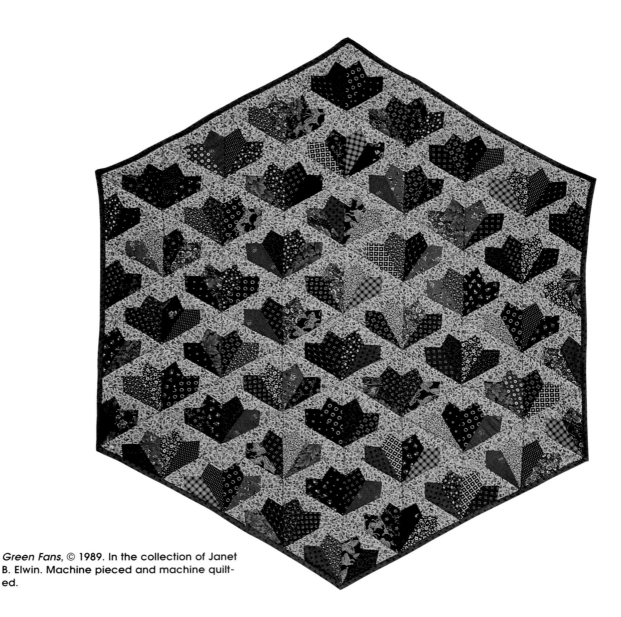

Green Fans, © 1989. In the collection of Janet B. Elwin. Machine pieced and machine quilted.

Stitch these two into the background pieces, then into a triangle set without being overly concerned about coordinating each and every piece. Finish all the triangle sets and arrange them into rows, just randomly putting the triangle sets into place according to the layout. After all the pieces are in place, go back and check each row so that you don't have two pieces of like fabric next to each other. This may be a little unnerving if you like to organize and coordinate each section, but I find the spontaneity of fabrics and patterns gives a bit of sparkle to the quilt. When you coordinate each section, you tend to use the fabrics you like best, leaving the not-so-pretty stuff out. By randomly choosing fabrics from your bag or box, you will use it all. Try this technique and see if you can relax a little about fabric selection.

TECHNIQUES

Straight Seam Sewing
Pivoting or Setting In
Using Coordinated and Blended Fabrics

LAYOUT AND CUTTING

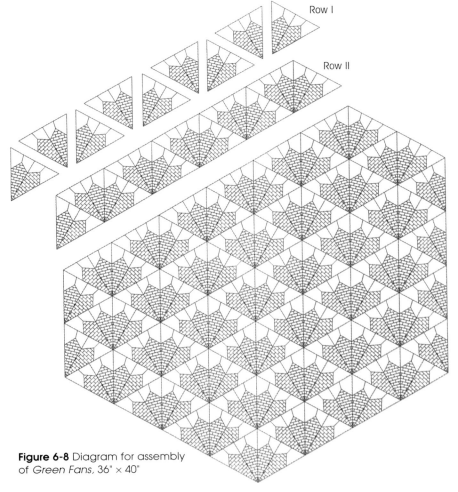

Row I

Row II

Figure 6-8 Diagram for assembly of *Green Fans*, 36" × 40"

Cutting Chart for *Green Fans*

	Fabric	Yardage	Template	# to Cut
Fans	24 Green prints	⅛ of each	A	8 of each
Background	Light or contrasting fabric	1	B C B reverse C reverse	96 96 96 96
Binding		¼		
Backing		1¼		

STITCHING SEQUENCE

1. Piece background sections together first, B to C and C reverse to B reverse.

2. Separate BC sections and C reverse/B reverse sections into piles.

3. Stitch fan A pieces into BC sections. Put aside.

4. Stitch fan A pieces into C reverse/B reverse sections. Put aside.

5. Stitch completed BC sections to C reverse/B reverse sections to make a triangle set as shown in Row I of Figure 6-8 (p. 67). Make 96 triangle sets.

6. Arrange triangle sets according to the layout in Figure 6-8. Stitch triangles together in rows (see Row II in Figure 6-8, p. 67) and join the rows.

QUILTING AND BINDING

Quilt in the ditch by machine. For binding instructions, see "Binding the Quilt" in Chapter 3.

Blue Dresden Plates

After I made *Green Fans* using just one fabric for the background, I wanted to experiment with blended fabrics. *Blue Dresden Plates* was the result.

TECHNIQUES

Straight Seam Sewing
Pivoting or Setting In
Using Coordinated and Blended Fabrics

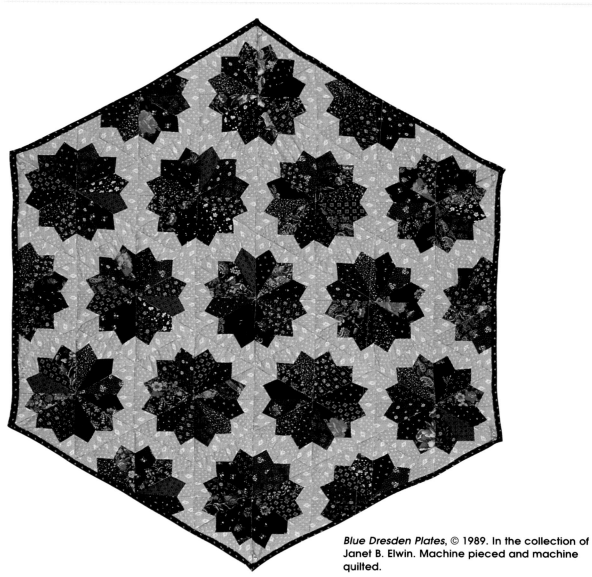

Blue Dresden Plates, © 1989. In the collection of Janet B. Elwin. Machine pieced and machine quilted.

LAYOUT AND CUTTING

	Fabric	Yardage	Template	# to Cut
Cutting Chart for *Blue Dresden Plates*				
Fans	24 Blue prints	⅛ of each	A	8 of each
Background	Beige pin dot	½	B	96
			C reverse	96
	Beige print	½	C	96
			B reverse	96
Binding		¼		
Backing		1¼		

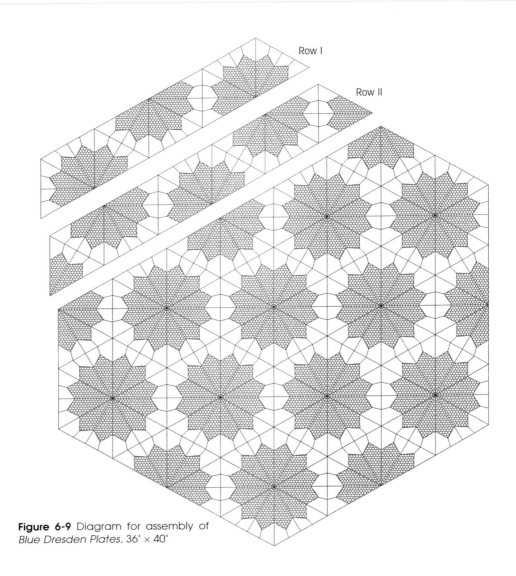

Figure 6-9 Diagram for assembly of *Blue Dresden Plates*, 36" × 40"

STITCHING SEQUENCE

1. Piece background sections together first, B to C and C reverse to B reverse.

2. Separate BC sections and C reverse/B reverse sections into piles.

3. Stitch fan A pieces into BC sections. Put aside.

4. Stitch fan A pieces into C reverse/B reverse sections. Put aside.

5. Stitch completed BC sections to C reverse/B reverse sections to make a triangle set. Make 96 triangle sets.

6. Arrange triangle sets according to the layout in Figure 6-9. Stitch triangles together in rows, as shown in Figure 6-9, and join the rows.

QUILTING AND BINDING

Quilt in the ditch by machine. For binding instructions, see "Binding the Quilt" in Chapter 3.

Return to Dresden

When I was invited to submit a challenge for the Silver Dollar City Show in 1990, I was already hooked on the all-pieced Dresden Plate pattern. My real challenge was to turn the project into a square. That is how I created this triangle background using four blended pink fabrics.

TECHNIQUES

Straight Seam Sewing
Pivoting or Setting In
Using Coordinated and Blended Fabrics
Making a Lattice
Piecing a Blended Background

Return to Dresden, © 1990. In the collection of Noriko Endo, Chiba, Japan. Made by Janet B. Elwin

Figure 6-10 Diagram for assembly of *Return to Dresden*, 36" × 36"

Cutting Chart for *Return to Dresden*

	Fabric	Yardage	Template	# to Cut
Fans	12 prints	⅛ of each	A	7 of each
Blended Background	Pink #1	1	B	42
			E	46
	Pink #2	1	C	42
			E	46
	Pink #3	1	B reverse	42
			E	46
	Pink #4	1	C reverse	42
			E	46
Lattice	Black	½	D	42
Binding		⅜		
Backing		1⅛		

STITCHING SEQUENCE

1. Piece background sections together first, B to C and C reverse to B reverse.

2. Separate BC sections and C reverse/B reverse sections into piles.

3. Stitch fan pieces into BC sections. Put aside.

4. Stitch fan pieces into C reverse/B reverse sections. Put aside.

5. Stitch completed BC sections to A reverse/B reverse sections to make a triangle set. Make 42 triangle sets.

6. Attach lattice D (made from Template D) to each set, lining notch marks on lattice to seam lines on triangle sets.

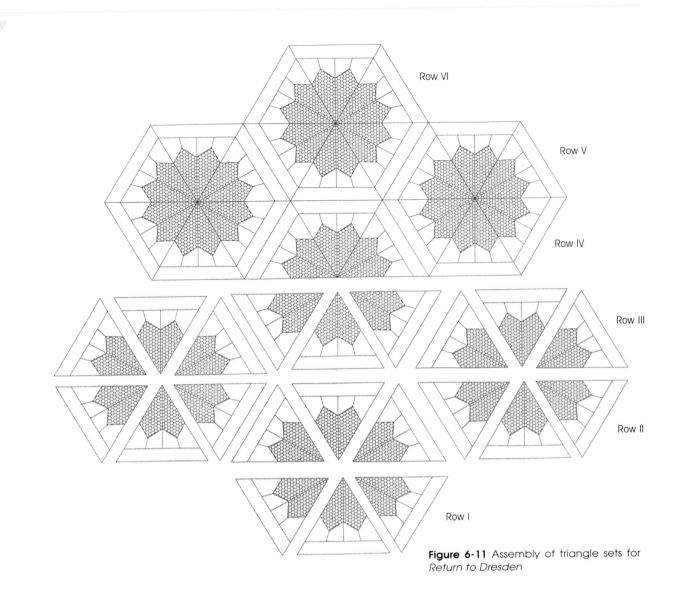

Row VI

Row V

Row IV

Row III

Row II

Row I

Figure 6-11 Assembly of triangle sets for *Return to Dresden*

7. Arrange triangle sets according to the layout shown in Figure 6-11. Stitch triangles together in rows from bottom to top, as shown in Figure 6-11, and join the rows.

8. Arrange background triangles (Template E) according to Figure 6-10 (p. 72). Stitch the units together and piece to the plates.

QUILTING AND BINDING

Quilt $\frac{1}{4}$" in around plates and triangles. Next, open a compass to $1\frac{1}{2}$" and draw a circle on template material. Cut this out and use as a template for the quilting pattern that will be centered in the middle of each plate. Mark the circle with a Clover Chaco-Liner (a brand name marker that washes out and comes in a variety of colors), then quilt.

For binding instructions, see "Binding the Quilt" in Chapter 3.

Necktie Quilt

Because the Fan and Dresden Plate quilts always remind me of neckties, I am adding this design which is made using neckties and shirting fabrics. I know this has nothing to do with triangles, but Gram's stitching technique for Dresden Plates is so easy, I wanted to include it for all of you. Of course, this can be done with all of your fabulous fabrics rather than neckties. I am showing you how to put this together in the traditional manner that Gram always used and that I have always taught my classes. Neckties are naturally made on the bias, so cut them on the bias. Cutting them on the straight of the grain would spoil the look.

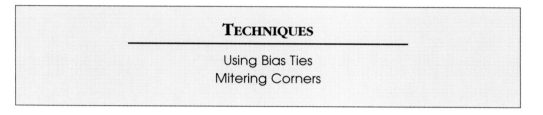

TECHNIQUES

Using Bias Ties
Mitering Corners

Necktie Quilt, © 1991. In the collection of Rosamund Champ, W. Sussex, United Kingdom. Made by Janet B. Elwin.

Cutting Chart for *Necktie Quilt*

	Fabric	Yardage	Template	Strip Size	# to Cut
Ties	Neckties	12 Ties	F (cut on solid lines)		7 from each tie
Background	Shirting #1	¾	G (lay on folded fabric)		7
	Shirting #2	¾	Half G H		4 6
Border	Tie-type print	¼ (1⅛ if cutting along selvage		5½" × 36½"	2
				5½" × 37"	2
Binding		⅜			
Backing		1⅛			

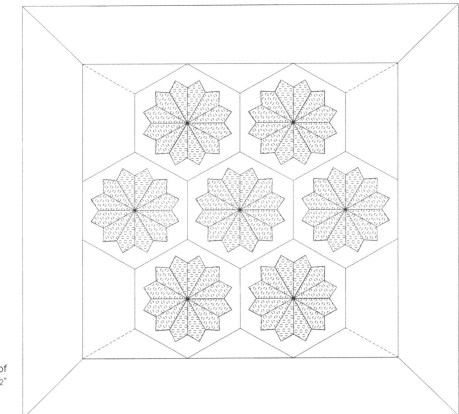

Figure 6-12 Diagram of *Necktie Quilt*, 35" × 36½"

STITCHING SEQUENCE

1. Fold each piece of tie fabric in half, right sides together.

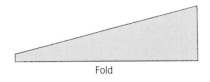

Figure 6-13 Tie fabric folded

Fold

2. Stitch across the wide end of the folded piece.

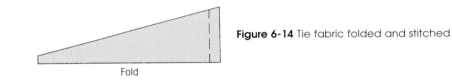

Figure 6-14 Tie fabric folded and stitched

Fold

3. Trim the point as shown in Figure 6-15.

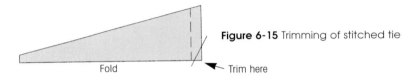

Figure 6-15 Trimming of stitched tie

Fold   Trim here

4. Turn, line seam up at center and press.

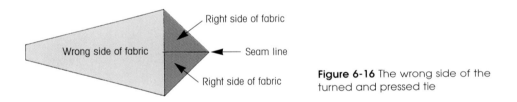

Right side of fabric

Wrong side of fabric   Seam line

Right side of fabric

Figure 6-16 The wrong side of the turned and pressed tie

5. Right sides together, stitch ties together two at a time along the long edges.

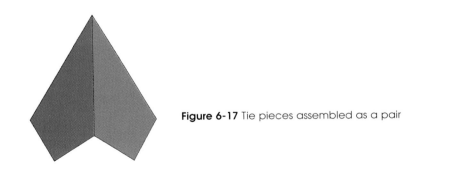

Figure 6-17 Tie pieces assembled as a pair

6. Arrange 12 ties (six pairs) in a circle. Divide each circle into an upper and lower half. To assemble the upper half, pin the center to the left pair, stitch them together, and finger press the seam to the left. Pin the right pair to the assembled section and stitch them together. Finger press the seam to the right.

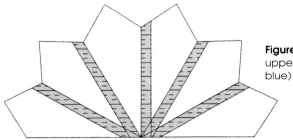

Figure 6-18 Wrong side of assembled upper half of tie motif (seams shown in blue)

7. Repeat Step 6 for the lower half. Pin the two halves together and stitch.

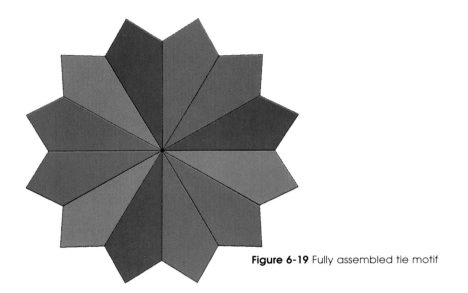

Figure 6-19 Fully assembled tie motif

8. To line up the tie motif on the hexagon background (Template G), you first must crease the hexagon into triangles (as indicated by dotted lines in Figure 6-20). To create triangle creases, iron the hexagon in half and then in thirds, matching edges.

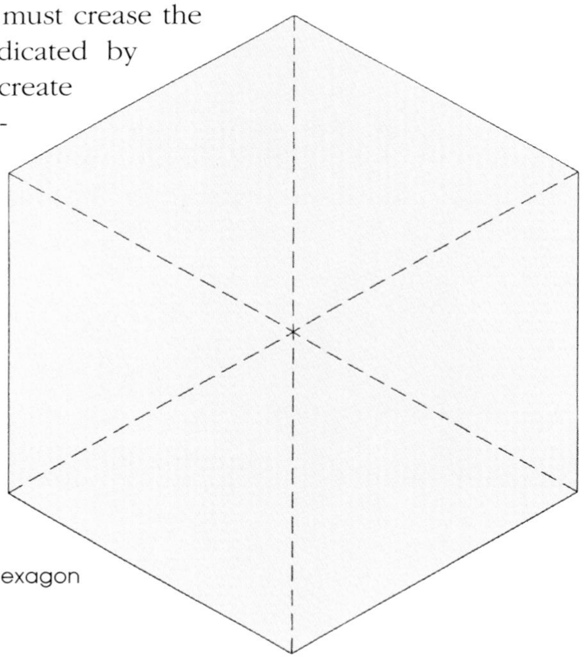

Figure 6-20 Creased hexagon

9. Adjust each necktie motif on top of the hexagon background so that the seams are along the hexagon creases. Pin the necktie motif in place. Either hand appliqué the motif in place or topstitch along the edge of the neckties.

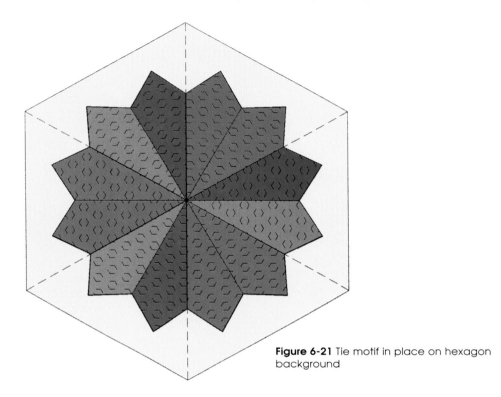

Figure 6-21 Tie motif in place on hexagon background

10. Piece necktie hexagon sections together. Then add background triangles and half hexagons.

11. Assemble borders. The $5\frac{1}{2}$" × $36\frac{1}{2}$" strips are side borders. The $5\frac{1}{2}$" × 37" strips are top and bottom borders. "Notch" each border by marking (with a pen or pencil) $5\frac{1}{4}$" in from each side. Mark the remainder of the strip into four equal sections.

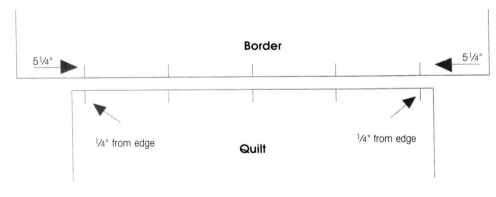

Figure 6-22 Notching of border and quilt edge

12. Pin the strip to the quilt, right sides together, matching marks and starting and ending ¼" from the edge. Stitch from pin to pin. Repeat for remaining sides.

13. Miter each corner by folding the quilt diagonally in half and laying the side strip over the top strip, right sides together, lining up the corner. Place a pin at the corner. Draw a diagonal line from the pin to the outside edge. Stitch along the line. Trim.

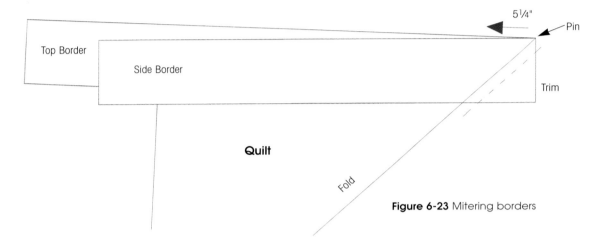

Figure 6-23 Mitering borders

QUILTING AND BINDING

Quilt in the ditch by machine. For binding instructions, see "Binding the Quilt" in Chapter 3.

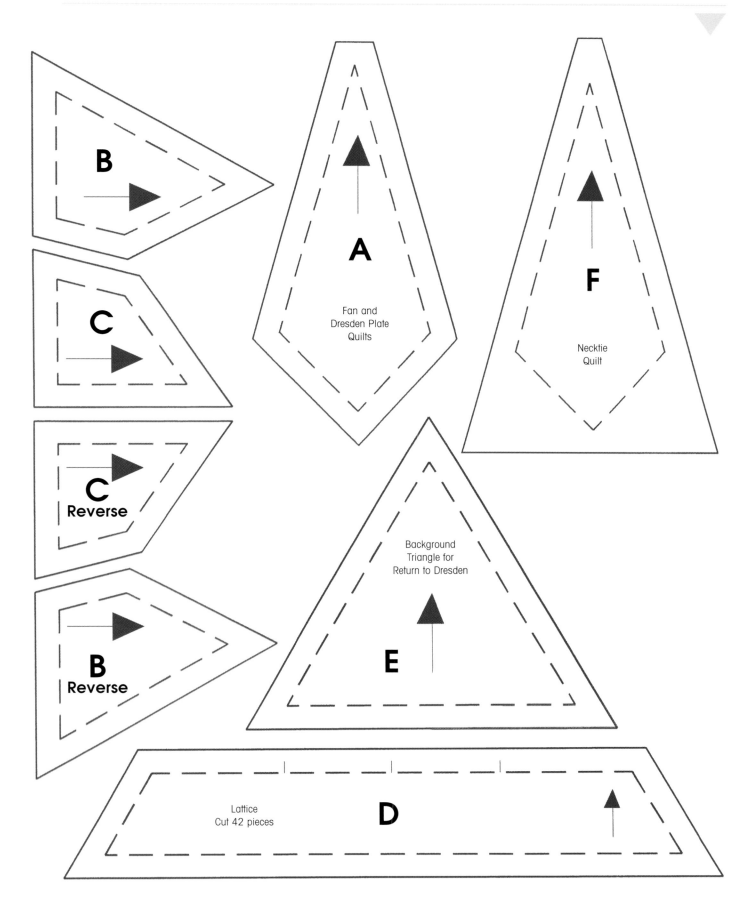

B

C

C
Reverse

B
Reverse

A

Fan and
Dresden Plate
Quilts

F

Necktie
Quilt

Background
Triangle for
Return to Dresden

E

Lattice
Cut 42 pieces

D

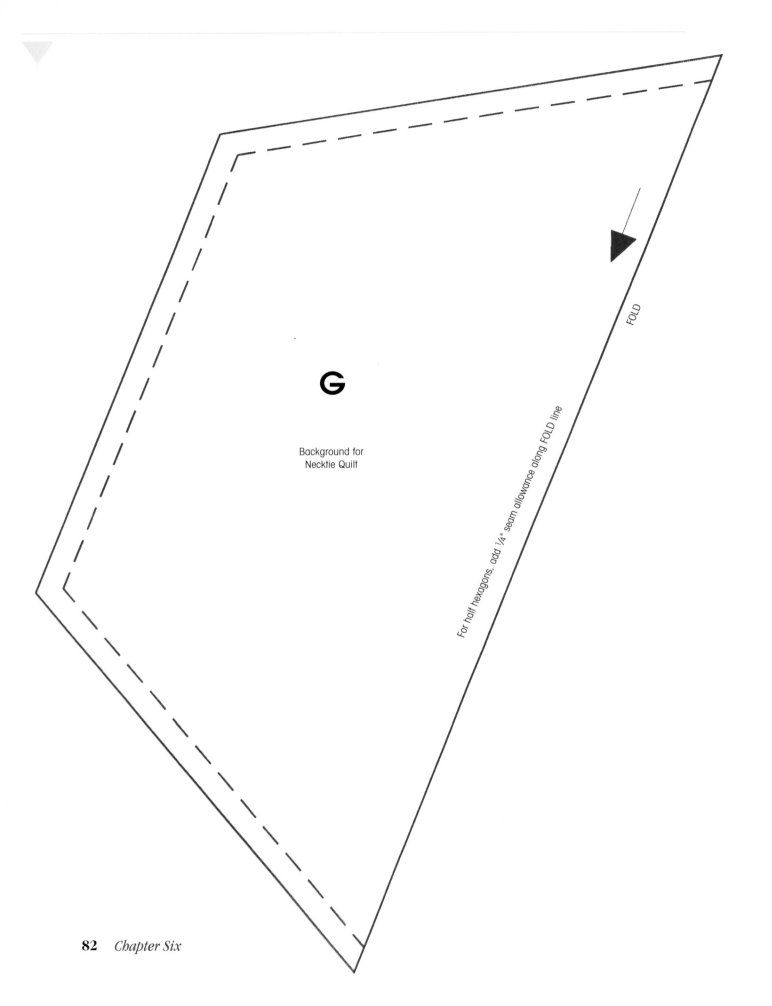

G

Background for
Necktie Quilt

FOLD

For half hexagons, add ¼" seam allowance along FOLD line

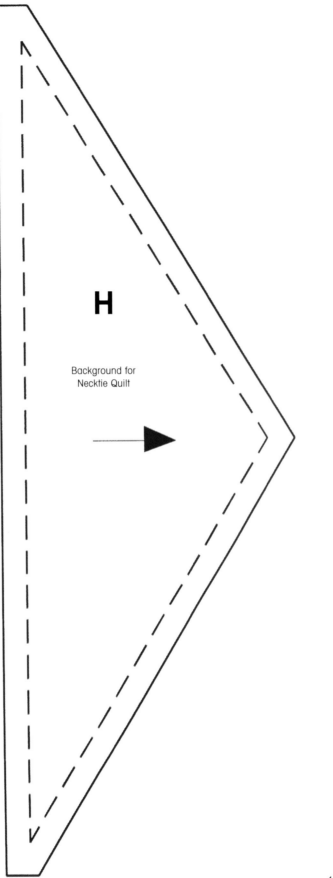

H

Background for
Necktie Quilt

Curves

In addition to working with the 60° angle, I also love to stitch and create designs using curves. I love the flow they give a pattern, often creating illusions. My very first quilts used patterns with curves. My first was a Double Wedding Ring and my second was the Orange Peel. I stitched both of these on the machine and had no trouble at all. I was fortunate in not having anyone tell me that some patterns were hard and others easy. Instead, I chose the ones I liked and worked on them. I really do think that if I had started out with just a very simple design and three coordinated pieces of fabric—the usual advice to beginners—I would have become bored quickly and might never have continued quilting. However, my first attempt was the Double Wedding Ring with scraps mostly bought at thrift shops. Remember, in the early '70s there weren't any quilt shops, and 100% cotton was a novelty. Because the cutting and sewing of quilts is so repetitive, it became a game to use as much fabric as I could in each section. This made it exciting to put the segments together. I am sure this theory still holds true for me today, because the more fabrics I can fit into a quilt, the happier I am.

It only stands to reason that eventually I would combine the curved seam into the 60°-angle design. This combination is very exciting and appealing, even for the beginner. One of the benefits of the 60°-angle curve is that it is so easy to sew. Just take a look at the square Drunkard's Path in Figure 7-1 and its 60° angle adaptation, *Windy Way*.

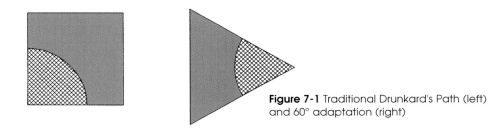

Figure 7-1 Traditional Drunkard's Path (left) and 60° adaptation (right)

Notice how deep the curve is in the square and how shallow it is in the 60° angle. It is truly like sewing a straight line. It couldn't be any easier. So, if you have been dying to try machine piecing curves, this next project is for you. There are several variations: a triangle and a rectangle quilt with no set color design, and a triangle and a rectangle quilt with a planned fabric design.

Windy Way

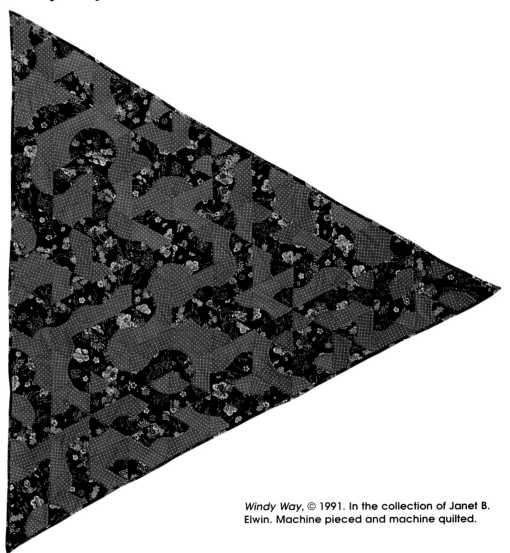

Windy Way, © 1991. In the collection of Janet B. Elwin. Machine pieced and machine quilted.

TECHNIQUES
Straight Seam Sewing
Using Contrasting Fabrics
Curved Seam Sewing

I have already told you that I like to make odd-shaped quilts. The triangular *Windy Way* certainly qualifies. By adding two triangle sections to the central triangle, however, you can make a more conventionally shaped rectangular quilt (see Figure 7-4, p. 88).

SEWING THE CURVES

1. Before you do any fabric selection or quilt planning, take Templates A and B at the end of this chapter and cut two pieces of fabric. Mark the notch inside the ¼" seam allowance. Do not cut the notch. The most important aspect of lining up the two pieces is matching the notches.

2. Pin the center notch first, as shown in Figure 7-2.

Figure 7-2 Assembling the 60° Drunkard's Path

3. Next, pin the right edge, then the left edge. Because the fabrics have been cut on the bias, there is plenty of ease. Just use three pins; the more pins you use, the more difficulties you will have. Stitch, with the curved triangle piece on top, from edge to edge. Press light toward dark. No need to clip. Easy!!!

LAYOUT AND CUTTING

When I made this quilt, I played and played on paper and couldn't quite come up with an arrangement I liked. I ended up using two contrasting fabrics, with half the units made up of light fabric for the concave pieces and dark fabric for the convex ones (a concave curve goes inward and a convex curve faces outward), while the other sets used dark

Figure 7-3 Diagram for *Windy Way* triangular quilt, 60" each side

Trim —→

Figure 7-4 Diagram for *Windy Way* rectangular quilt, 51" × 60". Top edge shows full Drunkard Path sets before they are trimmed to create a straight edge (bottom edge has already been trimmed).

fabric for the concave and light for the convex. Then I laid out the two types of sets and moved them around until I created a maze I liked. If you want to try that, make up 80 sets of each combination. This will give you a few extras of each set. The quilt could also be made up as a real scrap bag by using very dark darks or very light lights.

There are half sets along the top and bottom edge of the rectangular quilt. I think it is a lot easier to make whole sets, then trim, as shown in Figure 7-4.

Suggested Cutting Chart for *Windy Way*

	Fabric	Yardage	Template	# to Cut
Triangular Quilt	Light	1	A	75
			B	69
	Dark	1	A	69
			B	75
	Binding	3⁄8		
	Backing	2¼		
Rectangular Quilt	Light	2	A	155
			B	145
	Dark	2¼	A	145
			B	155
	Binding	3⁄8		
	Backing	3		

STITCHING SEQUENCE

1. Follow the directions given in "Sewing the Curves" earlier in the instructions for this quilt.

2. After stitching the sets together, arrange them according to Figure 7-4 (p. 88).

3. Stitch the sets together in rows.

4. *For the rectangular quilt only:* trim the top and bottom, leaving ¼" seam allowance.

QUILTING AND BINDING

Quilt in the ditch by machine. For binding instructions, see "Binding the Quilt" in Chapter 3.

Isn't it easy to work with 60°-angle curves? I bet you never thought you would be making a quilt using curves. Now that you have seen how easy it is, I'm sure you will be eager to try this next project.

BONUS PATTERN

Here is a design that I have used a lot when teaching my machine piecing class. Its curvy feel reminds me of an hourglass.

If you would like a traditionally set pattern, try the following.

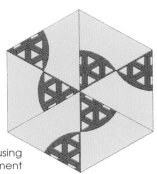

Figure 7-5 60° Drunkard's Path (made using Templates A and B) in hexagonal arrangement

Whirlwind

TECHNIQUES
Straight Seam Sewing Curved Seam Sewing

LAYOUT AND CUTTING

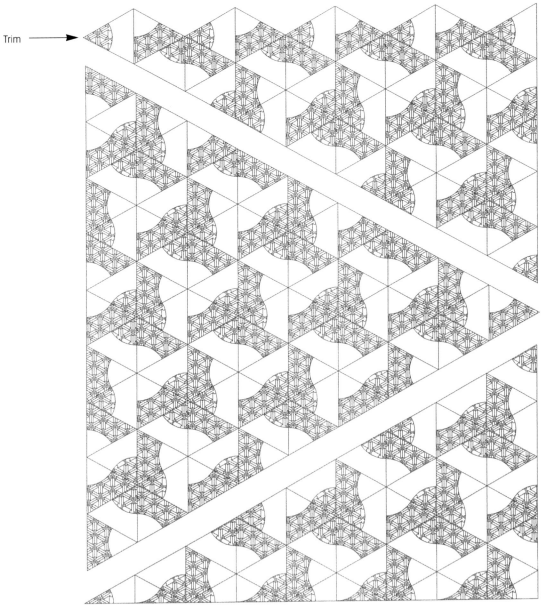

Trim →

Figure 7-6 Diagram for *Whirlwind* quilt. The triangular quilt (45" each side) is shown as the center piece of the rectangular layout. The top edge of the rectangular layout shows full Drunkard Path sets before they are trimmed to create a straight edge (bottom edge has already been trimmed). The rectangular quilt will be 38" × 45".

This looks as different as can be from *Windy Way*, but the sewing is the same in this repeat pattern. The patterned fabric in the diagram indicates the dark color.

Suggested Cutting Chart for *Whirlwind*

	Fabric	Yardage	Template	# to Cut
Triangular Quilt	Light	¾	A	45
			B	36
	Dark	¾	A	36
			B	45
	Binding	⅜		
	Backing	1⅜		
Rectangular Quilt	Light	1¼	A	85
			B	86
	Dark	1¼	A	86
			B	85
	Binding	⅜		
	Backing	1⅜		

STITCHING SEQUENCE

1. Arrange sets according to Figure 7-6.

2. Stitch in rows and join the rows.

3. *For the rectangular quilt only:* trim the top and bottom, leaving ¼" seam allowance.

QUILTING AND BINDING

Quilt in the ditch by machine. For binding instructions, see "Binding the Quilt" in Chapter 3.

Pond Lilies

Now that you are an expert on curves, I am going to show you an adaptation of my all-time favorite pattern—the simple curved triangle shown in Figure 7-7. It is used to make the *Pond Lilies* quilt.

Figure 7-7 Curved triangle used in *Pond Lilies* quilt

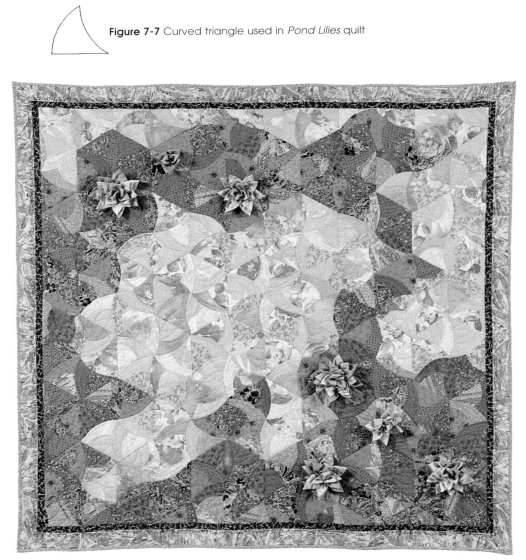

Pond Lilies, © 1991. In the collection of Janet B. Elwin. Machine pieced and machine quilted.

I have used the simple curved triangle in several quilts: *Tumbleweeds, Ocean Odyssey* and *The Stone Wall*. These have been featured in my book *Hexagon Magic* (EPM, 1986) as well as in quilting magazines. In *Tumbleweeds* I used the curve alone, in *Ocean Odyssey* I combined it with triangles, and in *The Stone Wall* I made hexagons with lattice work. This time I thought, why not divide it into two sections as in the Drunkard's Path? That way I could create more movement by using more fabrics.

Let's try it. Again, before you cut out the entire quilt, why don't you put one set together, using the instructions for "Sewing the Curves" on page 87 and Templates C and D at the end of this chapter. Don't give up on this pattern before you even begin. If you try it and don't like it, you can simplify the process by using my favorite curved triangle as one piece (refer to the footnote in the Cutting Chart for *Pond Lilies* on page 94). So just read on.

Try one set without including the seam allowance—just trace the pattern along the dotted lines. Don't forget to add the notch to each template. Try another set including the seam allowance.

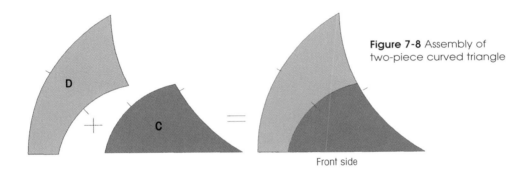

Figure 7-8 Assembly of two-piece curved triangle

Front side

This is one pattern where you cannot double-fold fabrics for cutting because that would create a mirror image. Instead, open the fabric and mark on the reverse side of it. If you like to cut several fabrics at once, open all fabrics and lay them one on top of the other, wrong sides up. After cutting the pieces, go back and mark the notches.

LAYOUT AND CUTTING

Don't let the diagram for this quilt scare you. If you could piece the *Windy Way* pattern, you can do this, too. The diagram (p. 95) shows the pond to which you will attach three-dimensional lilies. The patterned triangles represent the darker color of fabric.

This is a very muted "Monet"-style quilt with all the fabrics extremely closely related in color. Some are even blended. I wanted to make a very soft, peaceful-looking piece; one that could make you dream of warm, summer days. Your images of pond lilies may be different, so choose closely related and blended fabrics in your personal color field. I once made a pond lily quilt in dark greens.

Cutting Chart for *Pond Lilies*

	Fabric	Yardage	Template	Strip Size	# to Cut
Blended "Pond"	8 Light	¼ of each	C D or E*		15 of each 15 of each 15 of each
	11 Medium to dark	¼ of each	C D or E*		13 of each 13 of each 13 of each
Pond Lilies	Light	2½	F		160
Borders	Dark highlighter	¼ if cut crossgrain 1¾ if cut on grain**		See "Borders," p. 96	see "Borders," p. 96
	Second medium	½ if cut crossgrain 1¾ if cut on grain**		See "Borders," p. 96	see "Borders," p. 96
Binding		½			
Backing		2⅝			

*Because Template E (used for quilting later in this chapter) is the shape of Templates C and D sewn together, it can be used in their place. Using E instead of C and D results in less piecing and a quilt that still looks wonderful.

**Cut on-grain borders only if your fabric will not hide the piecing required to make crossgrain borders.

STITCHING SEQUENCE

1. Stitch all the light sets together, then all the dark sets. Again, notice that I have not had you cut half sets.

2. Lay out all the sets following the diagram in Figure 7-9. Move fabrics around until you have a pleasing arrangement.

3. Because there are so many curved edges in this design, the piecing cannot be done in rows. Referring to the set numbers in Figure 7-10, stitch the sets together into hexagon units as follows:

▼ Stitch set 1 to set 2 and finger press the seam to the left (away from the center set).

▼ Stitch the assembled 1-and-2 set to set 3, stitching set 1 to set 3. Finger press the seam to the right (away from the center set). This completes a half hexagon.

▼ Repeat for the other half of the hexagon.

Figure 7-9 Diagram for *Pond Lilies* quilt top, 56" × 58"

▼ Pin the two halves together, center first, then ends, then notches. Note that the notches are shown in Figure 7-8 (p. 93).

4. Stitch from edge to edge, then press.

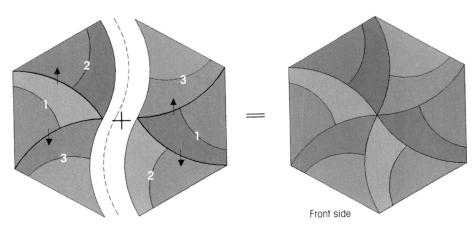

Front side

Figure 7-10 Assembly of *Pond Lilies* hexagon

5. After all the hexagon units are finished, pin them together in rows at their ¼" seam lines, as shown in Figure 7-11.

6. Sew each row, stitching only from pin to pin, leaving ¼" opening at top and bottom.

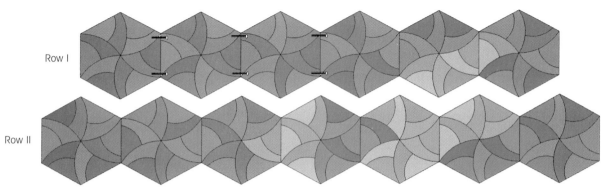

Figure 7-11 Assembling rows of *Pond Lilies* hexagons

7. Stitch row I to row II, pinning each unit right sides together to the unit in the previous row at the ¼" seam line. Stitch from pin to pin. You can try pivoting this, but I think it is easier in the long run to stitch from pin to pin. Stitch the remaining rows, then join the rows.

8. Add a pair of two-piece triangles to each open edge of the top and bottom sections of the quilt (the top section is shown in Figure 7-12). To create straight edges, trim the top, bottom, and sides of the quilt as indicated by the dotted lines in Figure 7-12.

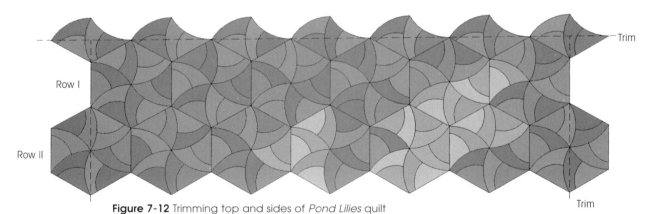

Figure 7-12 Trimming top and sides of *Pond Lilies* quilt

BORDERS

HIGHLIGHTER BORDER

1. *For crossgrain border only:* cut six strips the width of the fabric × 1¼". Stitch the strips together at the short ends, iron them, and continue with the remaining steps.

2. Cut two strips 1¼" × 56½". These will be the side strips.

3. Cut two strips $1\frac{1}{4}" \times 58\frac{1}{2}"$. These will be the top and bottom strips.

SECOND BORDER

1. *For crossgrain border only:* cut six strips the width of the fabric $\times$ $2\frac{1}{2}"$. Stitch the strips together at the short ends, iron them, and continue with the remaining steps.

2. Cut two strips $2\frac{1}{2}" \times 56\frac{1}{2}"$. These will be the side strips.

3. Cut two strips $2\frac{1}{2}" \times 58\frac{1}{2}"$. These will be the top and bottom strips.

PIECING AND ATTACHING BORDERS

1. Stitch each highlighter and corresponding second border piece together lengthwise, and treat them as one.

2. Notch each border by marking 3" in from either side of the $\frac{1}{4}"$ seam allowance. Mark the remainder of the strip into four equal sections.

3. Mark $\frac{1}{4}"$ in from either side of quilt edge. Mark the remainder of the quilt edge into four equal sections.

4. Pin the border strip to the quilt, matching notches. Stitch between pins at either end. Repeat for remaining sides.

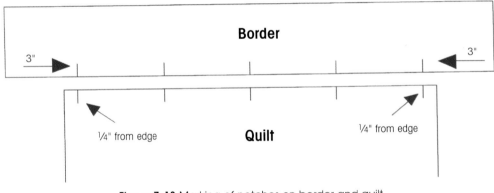

Figure 7-13 Marking of notches on border and quilt

5. Miter corners by folding the quilt diagonally in half and laying the top strip over the side strip, right sides together, lining up corners. Pin at intersection of seams. Draw a diagonal line from pin to edge. Stitch from pin to edge. Trim.

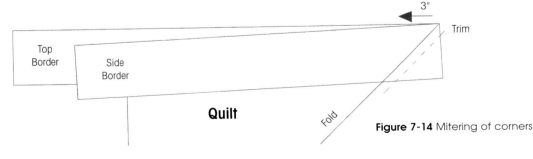

Figure 7-14 Mitering of corners

QUILTING AND BINDING

Quilt by machine in the ditch, then apply the over-quilting shown in Template E. I did this free-form by machine in each unit and extended the quilting into the border as far as it would go. The border is not the same size as the curved triangle unit, so the quilting template will not fit in the border. An additional quilted leaf design was added to the second border (Pattern #96 on my Pfaff Creative, 1475 CD). For binding instructions, see "Binding the Quilt" in Chapter 3.

MAKING AND ATTACHING THE POND LILIES

1. You will use Dune Points to make the three-dimensional pond lilies. Using Template F, make Dune Points following the directions in Figure 7-15. These are similar to making Prairie Points. Prairie Points use a square, but Dune Points use a hexagon shape, making a 60° angle when folded. Dune Points are only appropriate when making 60°-angle quilts.

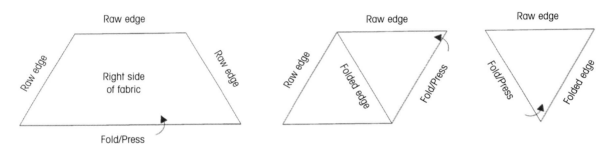

Figure 7-15 For each Dune Point, cut Template F from fabric and fold the piece in half, wrong sides together, as shown at left. Press the fold. Next, fold the piece so that the right bottom point meets the left top corner, shown at center. Press the new fold. Finally, fold the piece so that the left bottom point meets the right top corner, as shown at right. Press the new fold.

2. Stitch Dune Points together by overlapping them ¼". Use a zigzag stitch along the edge, catching a nylon thread in the stitching. You can then gather the points into a circle by pulling that thread. Stitch together 26 points to make a large lily, fewer to make a smaller lily, or more to make an even larger lily. Make approximately seven lilies of various sizes.

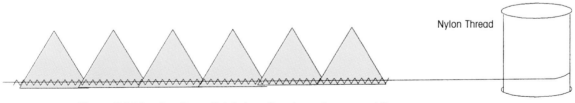

Figure 7-16 Sewing Dune Points together to make a pond lily

3. Appliqué the three-dimensional pond lilies to the quilt.

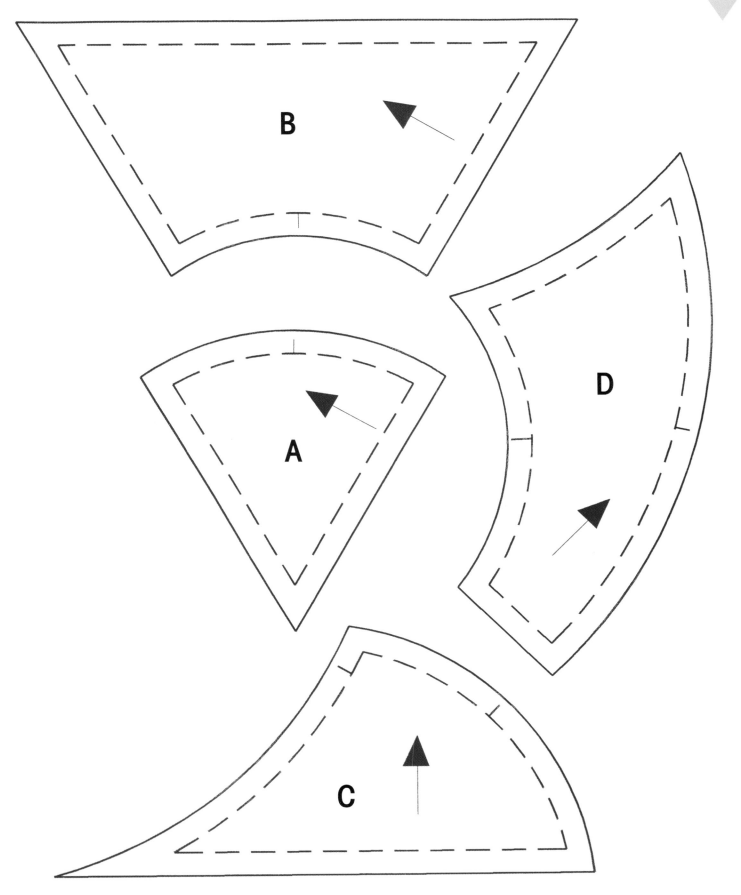

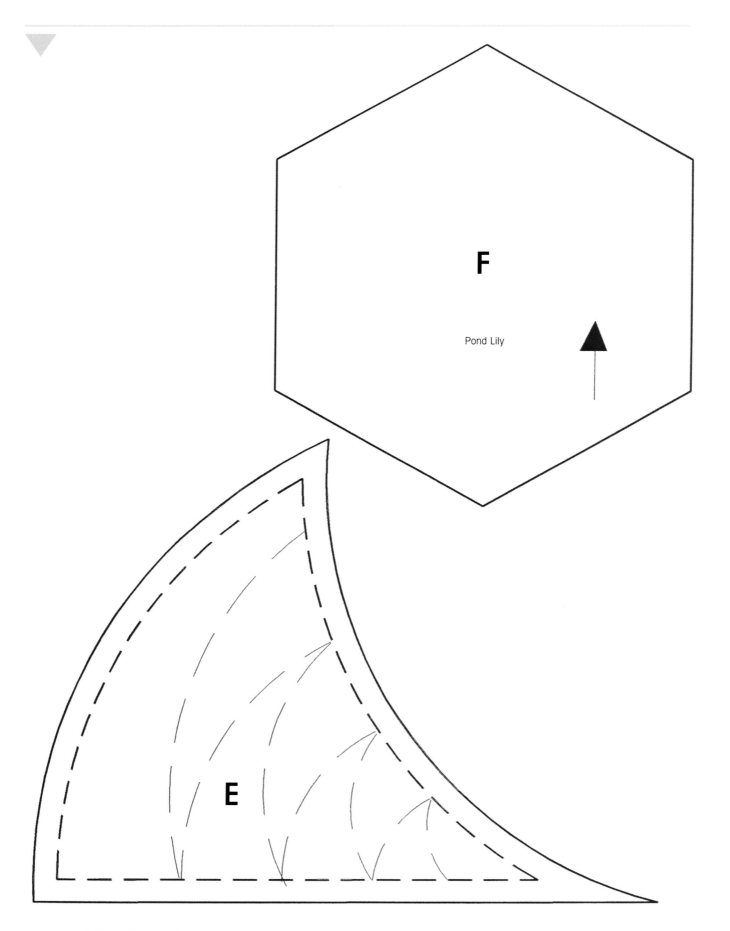

F

Pond Lily

E

Fractured Triangles

This technique packs a lot of punch. You can use it over and over again in any traditional design to give it a more contemporary feel. If you look at the color photo of *Hichinin Schimai* on page 103, at first glance you will recognize the familiar pattern called the Seven Sisters. But look again at each triangle. They are fractured into three sections. Not only that—each triangle can be turned three times to create a number of different designs for each star. In the diagram of *Hichinin Schimai* (p. 104), the triangles are not shown fractured because I didn't want to predetermine your arrangements of the stars. Just have fun playing with this technique and you will see the great potential for fracturing triangles in any pattern.

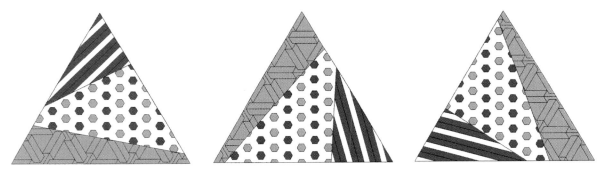

Figure 8-1 Three orientations of a fractured triangle

The design is something I suggested in Chapter 8 of my book *Hexagon Magic* (EPM, 1986). I never really thought I would do anything using what I then loosely called "abstract designs," but eventually my curiosity got the better of me. Tackling a huge pile of yellow fabrics, I made hundreds of triangles not knowing what the outcome would be. Midway through, I almost gave up, but all of a sudden a star emerged. I moved and moved the triangles around, and seven stars bounded forth. I was just amazed. Then I realized the unlimited potential for more "surprise" quilts by first combining fabrics and making triangles, then designing. For now, I will show you the process with a simplified version of my yellow *Australian Seven Sisters,* which is named after an aborigine story.

Australian Seven Sisters, © 1992. In the collection of Janet B. Elwin. Machine pieced and machine quilted

Hichinin Schimai

Hichinin Schimai, © 1993. In the collection of Janet B. Elwin. Machine pieced and machine quilted.

During a quilting trip to Japan, I collected some beautiful Japanese fabrics. In trying to decide how best to highlight them in a memory quilt, I chose the Seven Sisters pattern because I had taught in seven cities around that country. The name of this quilt is Japanese for seven sisters.

Figure 8-2 Diagram for *Hichinin Schimai,* 40" × 45" (fractured triangles not shown)

This diagram does not have specific fabric combinations drawn in. I am leaving it up to you and your imagination to arrange that yourself. The diagram looks like the traditional Seven Sisters, but yours will be fractured. Have fun with this fracturing. The possibilities are endless.

Cutting Chart for *Hichinin Schimai*

	Fabric	Yardage	Template	# to Cut
Star Set (1 set)	#1 and #2	⅛ of each	A	12
	#3	⅛ of each	B	12

Cutting Chart for *Hichinin Schimai* (continued)

	Fabric	Yardage	Template	# to Cut
Blended Background	Beige I	½	B	33
	Beige II	½	B	33
Large Background Triangle	Pale Green	⅝	See "Large Background Triangles," p. 107	2
Borders	Black highlighter	⅛	See "Borders," p. 108	See "Borders," p. 108
	Green	⅜	See "Borders," p. 108	See "Borders," p. 108
Binding		⅜		
Backing		1⅛		

The fabric yardage given on page 104 is for one star. The seven stars are made using a combination of strip piecing and templates. *Please read through all the directions before cutting any fabrics.* The seven stars are made up of three different fabric combinations. Some are blended and some have a little contrast. Put together seven different combinations using three fabrics (you'll need ⅛ yard of each fabric). Since the fabrics are numbered in sets of 1, 2, and 3, I have used Roman numerals I and II to define the background.

Color Suggestions for *Hichinin Schimai*

Star	Fabric Colors
Star 1	Brown, Green, Rust
Star 2	Two Rusts, Beige
Star 3	Three Greens
Star 4	Red/Gold, Gold, Beige/Gold
Star 5	Beige, Rust, Green
Star 6	Three Greens (different from Star 3)
Star 7	Yellow, Gold, Gray

STITCHING SEQUENCE

FOR EACH STAR

1. Cut one strip from fabric #1, 2¼" × the width of the fabric.

2. Cut one strip from fabric #2, 3¼" × the width of the fabric.

3. Sew the strips together lengthwise.

4. Press the seam allowance to one side. Press the front of the fabric also.

5. Using Template A on the reverse side of the fabric, align the guide line with the seam line.

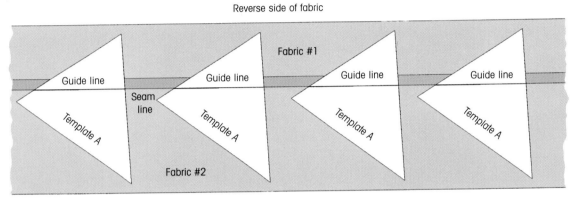

Figure 8-3 Aligning guide line of Template A with the seam line

6. Mark and cut 12 sets from the joined strips.

7. Cut one strip from fabric #3, 1¾" × the width of the fabric. You'll need another strip, 1¾" × half the width of the fabric. Stitch Template A sets, fabric #2 side, to fabric #3, for each strip, starting ¾" in from one end and allowing ¾" between each set. Press to either side.

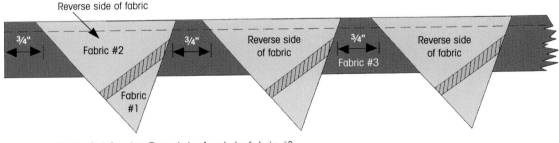

Figure 8-4 Sewing Template A sets to fabric #3

8. Mark the three fabrics that will create your 60° triangle with Template B, matching the guide line with the seam line between fabrics #2 and #3. Trace around the entire triangle and cut.

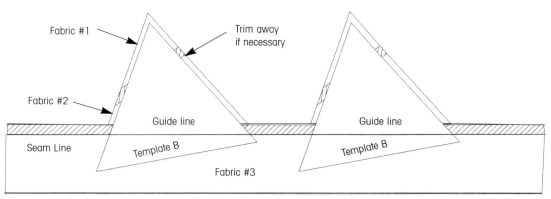

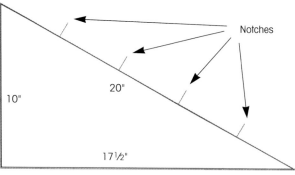

Figure 8-5 Marking pieced fabrics with Template B

9. On a flannel board or the floor (see p. 6), arrange each of the 12 sets to form a star. One way is to create a focal point in the center of each star by arranging the sets in a pattern. The second is to place the sets with no regard to design or pattern. The second alternative creates the "surprise"—a little spontaneity for me. Look at the picture of the quilt closely to see what I mean. The center star has a focal point and the rest are just randomly arranged. I have purposely not filled in the diagram in the hope that you will play and come up with your own individual star patterns.

10. Fill in the background beige I and II according to Figure 8-2 (p. 104).

11. Stitch by rows and join the rows.

LARGE BACKGROUND TRIANGLES

1. Tape together grid paper to make a piece big enough to draw the pattern shown in Figure 8-6. Put tracing paper over the grid and draw the pattern according to the measurements given.

Figure 8-6 Pattern for background triangles. Flip the pattern to create reverse triangles.

2. Mark notches every 4" along diagonal edge. Add seam allowance all around. Cut two triangles and two reverse triangles.

3. Line up the marked notches with the seams on triangles. Stitch the background triangle.

BORDERS

1. Cut four strips of the black highlighter fabric, 1" × the width of fabric.

2. Cut four strips of green, 2½" × the width of fabric.

3. Stitch the highlighter border to the green border along the long edges to make four 3"-wide lengths.

4. Cut two strips 35½" long from two of the lengths (these will be the sides).

5. Cut two strips 40½" long from the remaining lengths (these will be the top and bottom).

6. To make the corner blocks, stitch four blocks from leftover strip pieces according to Figure 8-7.

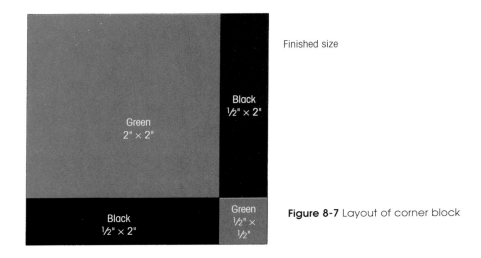

Finished size

Green
2" × 2"

Black
½" × 2"

Black
½" × 2"

Green
½" ×
½"

Figure 8-7 Layout of corner block

7. Stitch one block to either side of the top and bottom border strips.

8. Stitch the borders to the quilt, side borders first, then top and bottom. To ease the borders in place, mark the quilt and each border strip into quarters as explained in "Piecing and Attaching Borders" for the *Pond Lilies* quilt on page 97.

QUILTING AND BINDING

Quilt the free-hand "flower" of Template C in each of the stars. Quilt in the ditch for background and border. For binding instructions, see "Binding the Quilt" in Chapter 3.

EXPLORING FRACTURING OPTIONS

What I like so much about fracturing triangles is that you can take any traditional triangle pattern, fracture the triangles, and make a very contemporary-looking quilt, as in *Australian Seven Sisters* and *Hichinin Schimai.* You can also design something completely new, like the following quilt, *After the Hunt.* The options are limitless and so are the piecing methods. In *Hichinin Schimai,* we explored a strip piecing/template method that works very well if you have newly purchased fabric or so much yardage that you don't mind straightening a piece that you have previously cut into. Let me offer you two other options for fracturing triangles that work well if you have bits and pieces of fabrics or some fairly good-sized chunks that are not big enough for strip piecing.

FRACTURING OPTION *I*

This is the strip piecing and template method used in *Hichinin Schimai* (see pages 106–107). It results in repetitive sets.

FRACTURING OPTION *II*

This method uses separate templates for each fabric. If you use this option, which is how I did *Australian Seven Sisters,* you can mix and match your fabrics and not have a repetitive set in the batch. Even using only three different fabrics, you can arrange them in at least three different ways. Make three separate templates, 1, 2, and 3, from Template D at the end of this chapter. Be sure to add seam allowance all around.

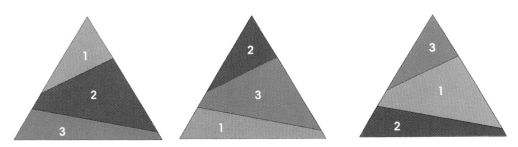

Figure 8-8 Fractured triangle variations with three fabrics

FRACTURING OPTION *III*

This method involves stitching the fabrics to paper templates. This is great for using up small pieces of fabrics (save all those scraps you have been tossing out) and again will give you a great mix. This option, often called machine paper piecing, is very accurate. Use Template D to create a paper base for this technique.

1. Photocopy Template D. For an accurate photocopy, trace the pattern onto a sheet of paper. The paper will lie flat in the copy machine, whereas the binding of a book will not allow the paper to lie flat and will cause distortion. Make as many copies as needed for your quilt project. Cut excess paper away.

2. Hold the paper up to the light with the lines facing toward you. Cover the center space (fabric area #1) with a piece of fabric, wrong side down, at least ½" bigger all around. Pin the fabric in place.

3. Turn over the paper and stitch on the lines surrounding fabric area #1.

4. Cover fabric area #2 with a piece of fabric, wrong side down, at least ½" bigger all around.

5. Flip the fabric over so that it is on top of the first fabric, right sides facing. Stitch along the line between fabric areas #1 and #2. Open up the second fabric.

6. Repeat Steps 4 and 5 for fabric area #3.

7. Iron the fabric while it is still attached to the paper.

8. Trim all seams to ¼" seam allowance.

9. Tear away the paper.

All these options take about the same amount of time. It is just a matter of how much fabric you have and/or what you would like the end result of your quilt to be. I have used all three and will probably continue to do so, depending on whether I want a repetitive block or one that is scattered.

In *After the Hunt,* I will give the directions again for the first option, because this is a technique that you may not have used before and that I developed for this book.

After the Hunt

After the Hunt, © 1993. In the collection of
Janet B. Elwin. Machine pieced and
machine quilted.

TECHNIQUES

Straight Seam Sewing
Strip Piecing/Template Making
Setting In
Using Contrasting, Blended, and Coordinated Fabrics
Doing Random and Pattern Quilting

LAYOUT AND CUTTING

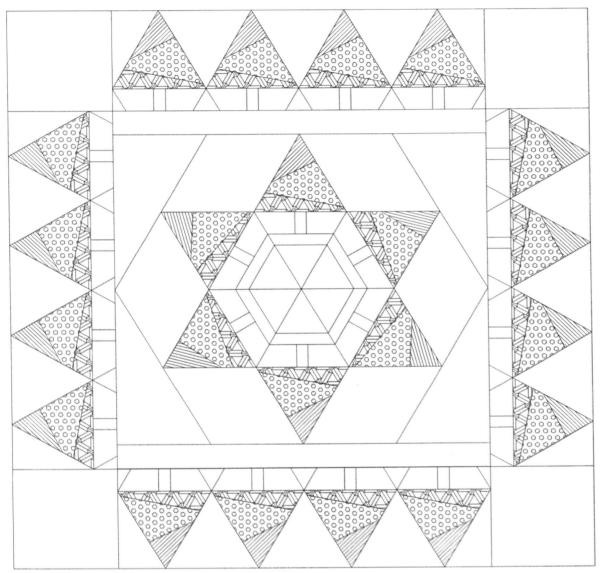

Figure 8-9 Diagram for *After the Hunt,* 25" × 25"

In the color photo of *After the Hunt,* notice that the fracturing in the trees is randomly arranged, while in the diagram it is all in one direction. Either is acceptable; just aim for a pleasing effect.

Cutting Chart for *After the Hunt*

	Fabric	Yardage	Template	# to Cut
Trees	3 Fabrics*	¼ of each	A	22
			B	22
Background	White	½	B	12
			Half B	4
			Half B reverse	4
			E	22
			E reverse	22
			J	6
	Stripe	¼	G	6
			I	12
			Half I	4
			Half I reverse	4
			K	2
			K reverse	2
			1½" × 16½" strips	2
Tree Trunks	Brown	⅛	F	22
Center Triangles	Print	¼	H	6
Corner Blocks	Print		5" × 5" blocks	4
Binding		¼		
Backing		¾		

* My trees are Christmas trees in holiday colors, but they could be trees in any season or a mix of seasons.

STITCHING SEQUENCE

TREES

1. Assemble 22 fractured triangles according to the stitching sequence "For Each Star" on pages 106–107. Set aside 16 triangles for the border.

2. Stitch background E to trunk F to background E reverse, making 22 sets. Set aside 16 sets for the border.

Figure 8-10 Piecing of trunk F to background E and E reverse

3. Stitch only six of the backgrounds from Step 2 to six of the fractured triangles from Step 1. Set aside. These are for the center. The border trees are put together differently as described later in the instructions.

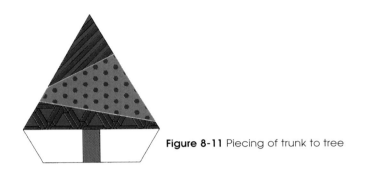

Figure 8-11 Piecing of trunk to tree

CENTER

1. Stitch together pieces G and H. Attach this combined piece to a tree section. Repeat for each tree section until you have six diamonds.

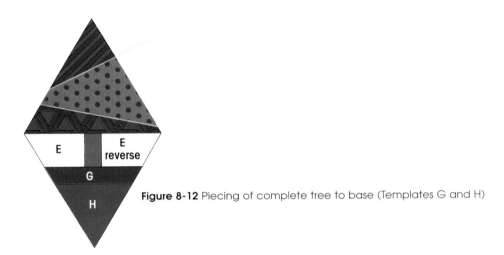

Figure 8-12 Piecing of complete tree to base (Templates G and H)

2. Piece the tree diamonds together, following Figures 8-9 (p. 111) and 8-13.

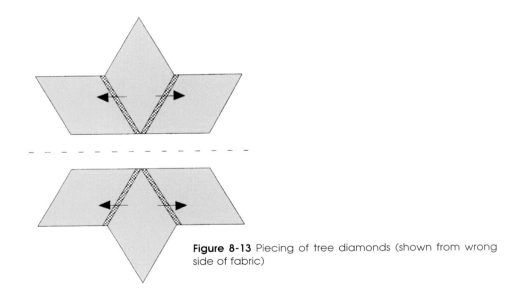

Figure 8-13 Piecing of tree diamonds (shown from wrong side of fabric)

3. Pivot or set in the background diamonds, made from Template J. Both the pivot and set-in techniques are discussed in Chapter 5 (pp. 52–53).

SQUARING IT UP

1. Stitch the triangles cut from Template K onto four sides of the hexagonal center to make it a rectangle. Consult Figure 8-9 on page 111.

2. Add a striped background strip to the top and bottom, making the center a 16" square.

TREE BORDER

1. Stitch a background B to a fractured triangle tree to a background B, and so on, to make row I as shown in Figure 8-14. Press seams to one side.

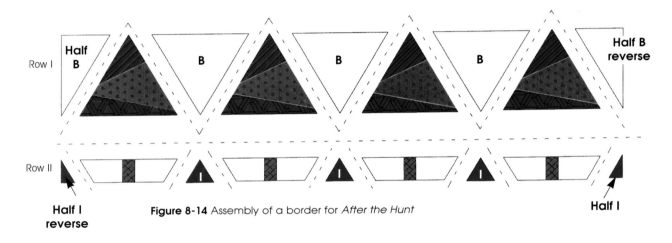

Figure 8-14 Assembly of a border for *After the Hunt*

2. Stitch a background I to a pieced trunk to a background I, and so on, to make row II as shown in Figure 8-14. Press seams to one side.

3. Stitch row I to row II, matching intersections, to make a border. Repeat for the remaining three borders.

4. Set two of the borders aside. Add two corner blocks to each side of the top and bottom borders.

5. Stitch side borders to quilt.

6. Stitch top and bottom borders to quilt.

QUILTING AND BINDING

I machine quilted random swirls over the entire quilt top. Occasionally, I varied my straight quilting stitch with a machine-programmed snowflake stitch (stitch #159 on Pfaff Creative 1475). For binding instructions, see "Binding the Quilt" in Chapter 3.

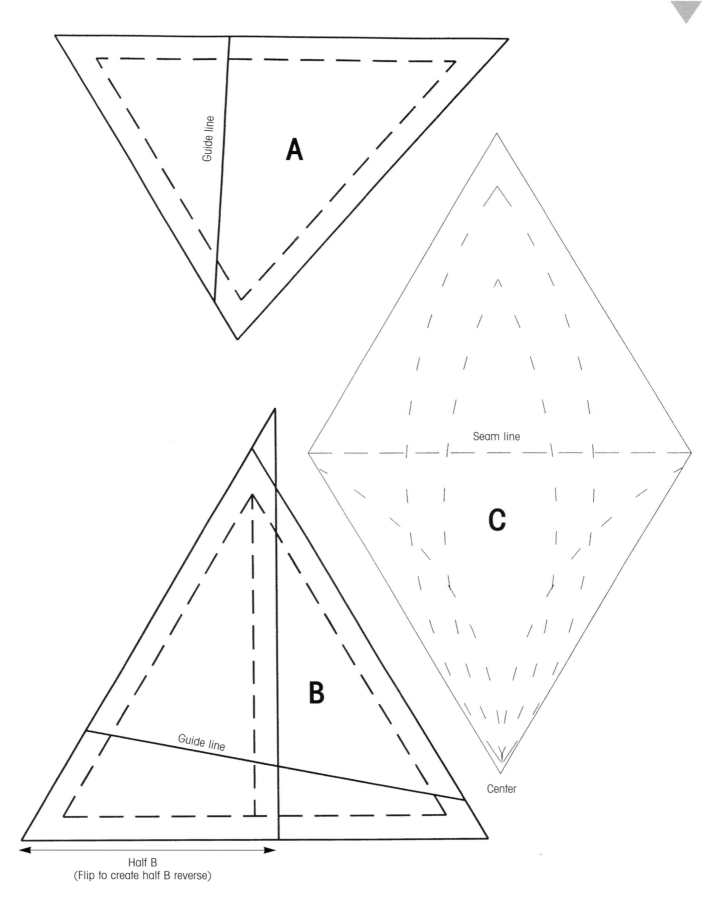

Guide line

A

Seam line

C

Center

Guide line

B

Half B
(Flip to create half B reverse)

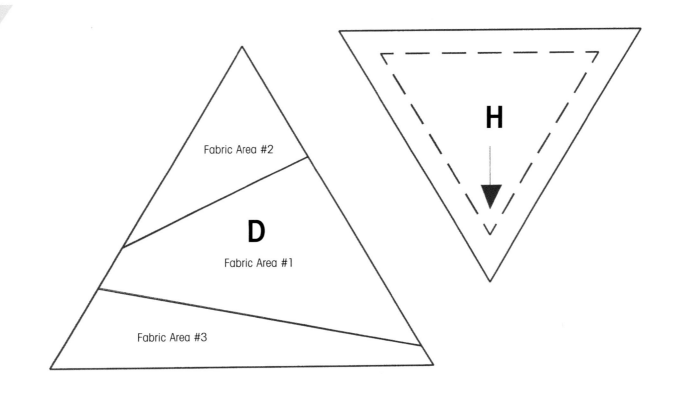

Fabric Area #2

D

Fabric Area #1

Fabric Area #3

H

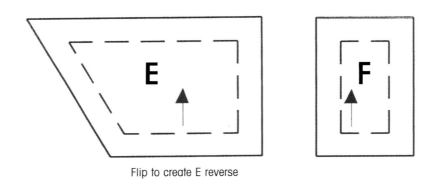

E

Flip to create E reverse

F

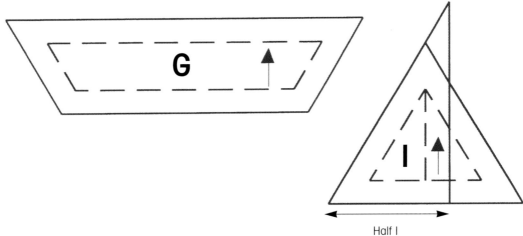

G

I

Half I
(Flip to create half I reverse)

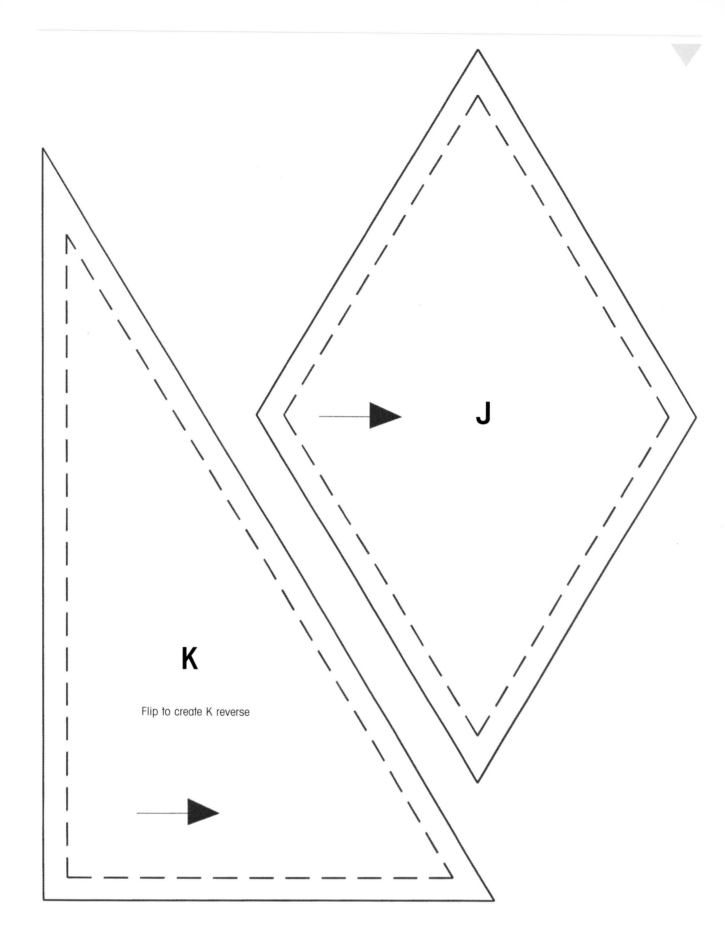

K

Flip to create K reverse

J

More Triangles

Here are a couple of quilts with triangles shaped a little differently. *Fly-A-Way* is a design that I simplified from a hexagon-shaped pattern in my book *Hexagon Magic* (EPM, 1986) called *The Birds*. This version is made with triangle sets.

Fly-A-Way

TECHNIQUES

Straight Seam Sewing
Setting in or Pivoting
Using Coordinated Fabrics

We love to feed the birds and have six feeders hanging from our deck. There are times when it looks like rush hour at the airport with all the flying around. This quilt represents just some of the birds that come to our feeders.

LAYOUT AND CUTTING

You have used all the sewing techniques needed for this quilt in previous projects in this book. The pieces can be either pivoted or set in. The yardage is calculated by using only one fabric for each of the light, medium, and dark triangles. I used scraps, and you may have enough bits and pieces to do the same.

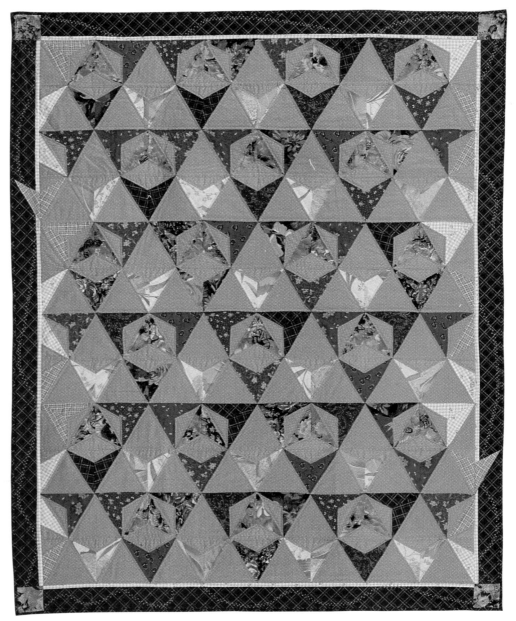

Fly-A-Way, © 1992. In the collection of Janet B. Elwin. Machine pieced and machine quilted.

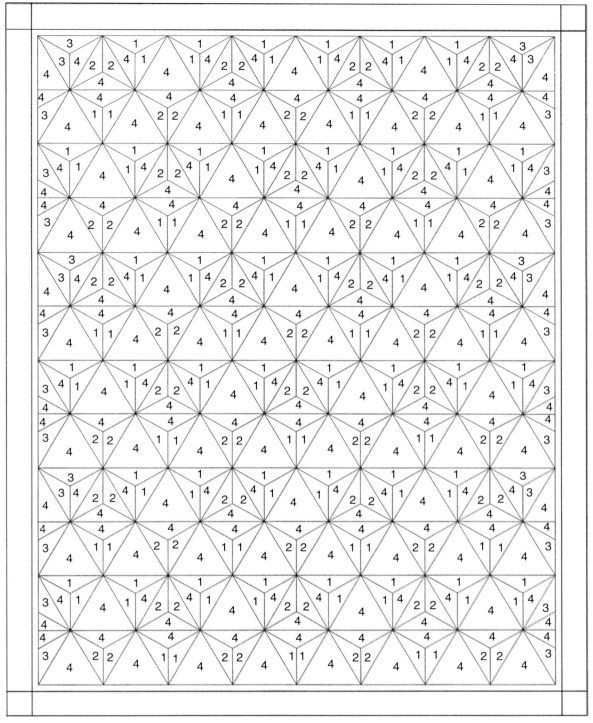

Figure 9-1 Diagram for *Fly-A-Way*, 45" × 56"

Cutting Chart for *Fly-A-Way*

	Fabric	Yardage	Template	Strip Size	# to Cut
Birds	#1 Dark	½	A		126
	#2 Medium	¼	A		84
	#3 Light	¼	A		30
Background	#4	1	Half A		9
			Half A reverse		9
			B		68
			Half B		3
			Half B reverse		3
Borders	Gray highlighter	¼		1" × 40½"	2
				1" × 51½"	2
	Rust	¼		2½" × 40½"	2
				2½" × 51½"	2
Corners	Print	⅛		3" × 3"	4
Binding		⅜			
Backing		1¾			

STITCHING SEQUENCE

1. Sew 63 of the set shown in Figure 9-2.

Figure 9-2 First triangle set for *Fly-A-Way*

2. Sew 42 of the set shown in Figure 9-3.

Figure 9-3 Second triangle set for *Fly-A-Way*

3. Sew six of the set shown in Figure 9-4.

Figure 9-4 Third triangle set for *Fly-A-Way*

4. Sew nine of the half set shown in Figure 9-5.

Figure 9-5 Fourth triangle set for *Fly-A-Way*

5. Sew nine of the half reverse set shown in Figure 9-6.

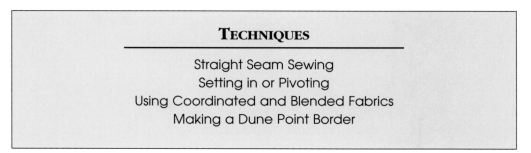

Figure 9-6 Fifth triangle set for *Fly-A-Way*

6. After assembling the triangle sets, lay them out on a flannel board according to Figure 9-1 (p. 121), and then stitch them together by rows.

BORDERS

Reminder: When using ¼ yard pieces of fabric, cut crossgrain strips the required width, stitch the highlighter to the other border, and then cut this length as one piece. When the length needed is longer than 44" (or the width of the fabric), cut crossgrain strips and piece them to achieve the required length. This works just fine in most print fabrics. Otherwise, you will have to buy fabrics the length of the longest strip which is 51½", or 1½ yards.

After the border strips have been pieced, stitch the borders on and then appliqué two light triangles, one on each side border, as shown in the color photo on page 120.

QUILTING AND BINDING

Quilt in the ditch by hand. The border has a decorative stitch, done by machine, that looks like bird tracks (#48 on Pfaff Creative 1475 CD). For binding instructions, see "Binding the Quilt" in Chapter 3.

Hot Flashes

TECHNIQUES
Straight Seam Sewing
Setting in or Pivoting
Using Coordinated and Blended Fabrics
Making a Dune Point Border

Hot Flashes, © 1993. In the collection of Janet B. Elwin. Machine pieced and machine quilted.

If you get a chuckle from the name of this quilt, you have traveled down this same road. It seems that every occasion, except this one, is marked by quilting designs and patterns. There are so many "statement" quilts, but none to mark such a significant passage in a woman's life. As I am going through this transition now, I would like to honor or make light of the occasion.

LAYOUT AND CUTTING

The kite shape can easily be set in or pivoted into triangle sets, then pieced in rows. Of course, you don't have to make this a *Hot Flashes* quilt with these colors. Each "flash" is a combination of four fabrics, and even though the light

Figure 9-7 Diagram for *Hot Flashes*, 56" × 74"

background looks like the same fabric, it is three blended drapery prints. Have fun with this design, no matter what color flashes you work with. Check the diagram, which is color numbered to guide you (the print in the diagram represents the dark and medium colors).

Cutting Chart for *Hot Flashes*

	Fabric	Yardage	Template	# to Cut
Flashes Combination #1	Orange #1	⅛	D	6
	Orange #2	⅛	D	6
	Orange #3	⅛	D	6
	Orange #4	⅛	D	12
Flashes Combination #2	Orange/purple #1	⅛	D	6
	Orange/purple #2	⅛	D	6
	Orange/purple #3	⅛	D	6
	Purple #4	⅛	D	12
Flashes Combination #3	Magenta #1	⅛	D	6
	Magenta #2	⅛	D	6
	Purple #3	⅛	D	6
	Purple #4	⅛	D	12
Flashes Combination #4	Red #1	⅛	D	6
	Red #2	⅛	D	6
	Red #3	⅛	D	6
	Red #4	⅛	D	12
Flashes Combination #5	Purple #1	⅛	D	6
	Purple #2	⅛	D	6
	Dark Purple #3	⅛	D	6
	Dark Purple #4	⅛	D	12
Flashes Combination #6	Magenta #1	⅛	D	6
	Magenta #2	⅛	D	6
	Turquoise #3	⅛	D	6
	Turquoise #4	⅛	D	12
Flashes Combination #7	Burgundy #1	⅛	D	6

Cutting Chart for *Hot Flashes* (continued)

	Fabric	Yardage	Template	# to Cut
Flashes Combo #7 (cont.)	Burgundy #2	⅛	D	6
	Purple #3	⅛	D	6
	Purple #4	⅛	D	12
Light Background	3 Blended pale pinks, #5, #6, #7	⅞ of each	D	66 of each
Dark Background	Purple print #8	⅝	D Half D Half D reverse	44 12 12
	Plaid #9	¾	D	56
	Plaid #10	¾	D	56
Rectangle Edge	Plaid #9	¾	E	16
	Plaid #10	¾	E	16
Dune Points	2 Coordinating fabrics	1 of each	D	70 of each
Backing		3¼		

STITCHING SEQUENCE

1. For each of the seven fabric combinations, stitch the following sets.

▼ Stitch three of the set shown in Figure 9-8.

Figure 9-8 First triangle set for *Hot Flashes*

▼ Stitch three of the set shown in Figure 9-9.

Figure 9-9 Second triangle set for *Hot Flashes*

▼ Stitch two of the set shown in Figure 9-10.

Figure 9-10 Third triangle set for *Hot Flashes*

▼ Stitch two of the set shown in Figure 9-11.

Figure 9-11 Fourth triangle set for *Hot Flashes*

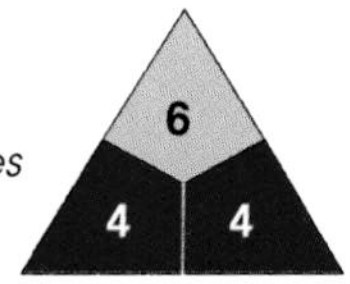

▼ Stitch two of the set shown in Figure 9-12.

Figure 9-12 Fifth triangle set for *Hot Flashes*

2. For the light background, stitch 52 of the set shown in Figure 9-13.

Figure 9-13 Light background set for *Hot Flashes*

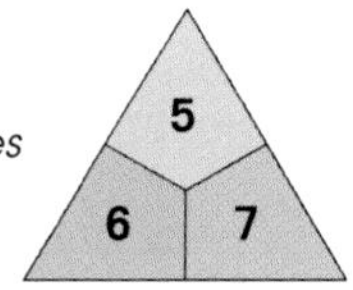

3. For the dark background, stitch the following sets.

▼ Stitch 44 of the set shown in Figure 9-14.

Figure 9-14 First dark background set for *Hot Flashes*

▼ Stitch 12 of the set shown in Figure 9-15.

Figure 9-15 Second dark background set for *Hot Flashes*

▼ Stitch 12 of the set shown in Figure 9-16.

Figure 9-16 Third dark background set for *Hot Flashes*

4. For the rectangle edge, stitch two of the set shown in Figure 9-17.

Figure 9-17 Rectangle edge set for *Hot Flashes,* created using Template E

5. Arrange all of the sets according to Figure 9-7 (p. 125), stitch the sets together in straight rows, and join the rows.

6. Stitch a rectangle edge to the top and bottom of the quilt.

DUNE POINTS

1. The folding instructions in Figure 9-18 are the same as for the pond lilies created in Chapter 7 (p. 98).

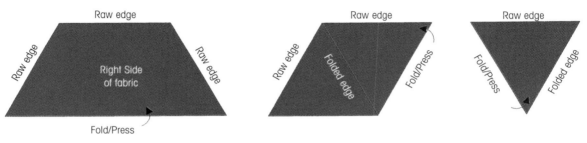

Figure 9-18 Folding of Dune Points. For each Dune Point, cut Template C from fabric and fold the piece in half, wrong sides together, as shown at left. Press the fold. Next, fold the piece so that the right bottom point meets the left corner, as shown at center. Press the new fold. Finally, fold the piece so that the left bottom point meets the right top corner, as shown at right. Press the new fold.

2. Stitch the Dune Points to the edge of the quilt.

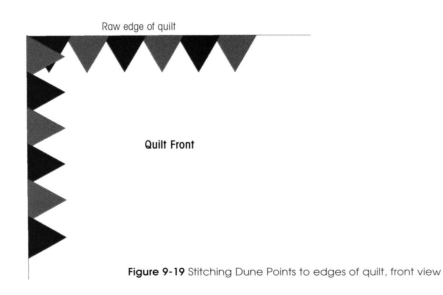

Figure 9-19 Stitching Dune Points to edges of quilt, front view

3. Turn the Dune Points to the outside of the quilt to create the border.

4. Trim the quilt backing to $\frac{1}{4}$" beyond the quilt edge, turn it under, and hem.

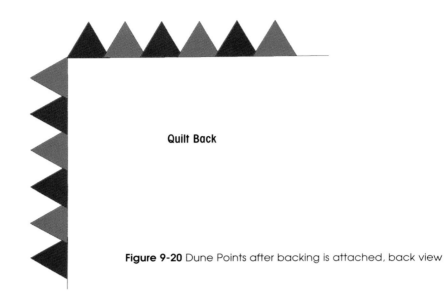

Quilt Back

Figure 9-20 Dune Points after backing is attached, back view

QUILTING AND BINDING

When quilting *Hot Flashes* I used a number of different programmed stitches to reflect my menopausal moods. Create a personal statement with your quilting. For binding instructions, see "Binding the Quilt" in Chapter 3.

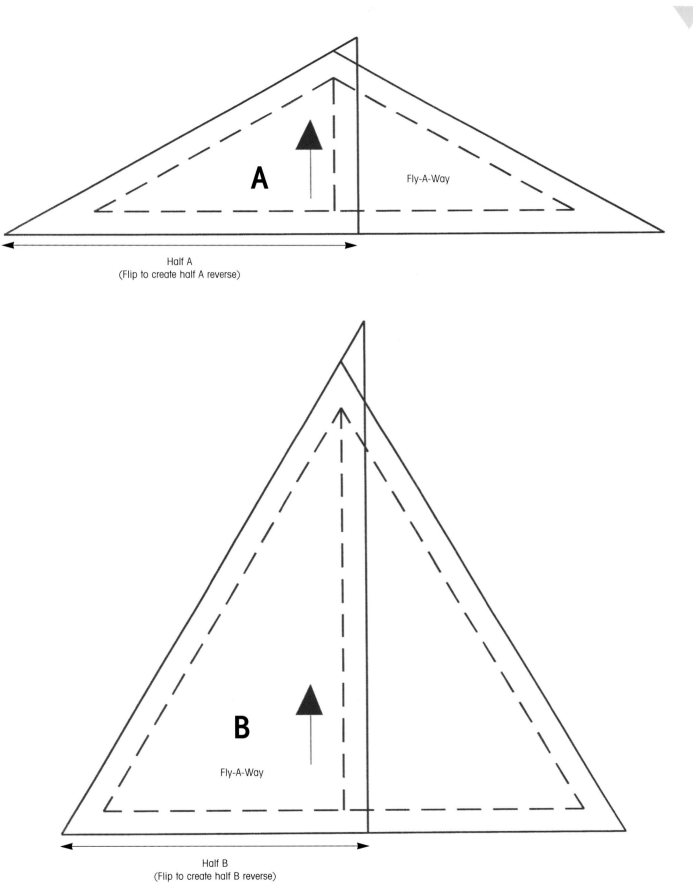

A

Fly-A-Way

Half A
(Flip to create half A reverse)

B

Fly-A-Way

Half B
(Flip to create half B reverse)

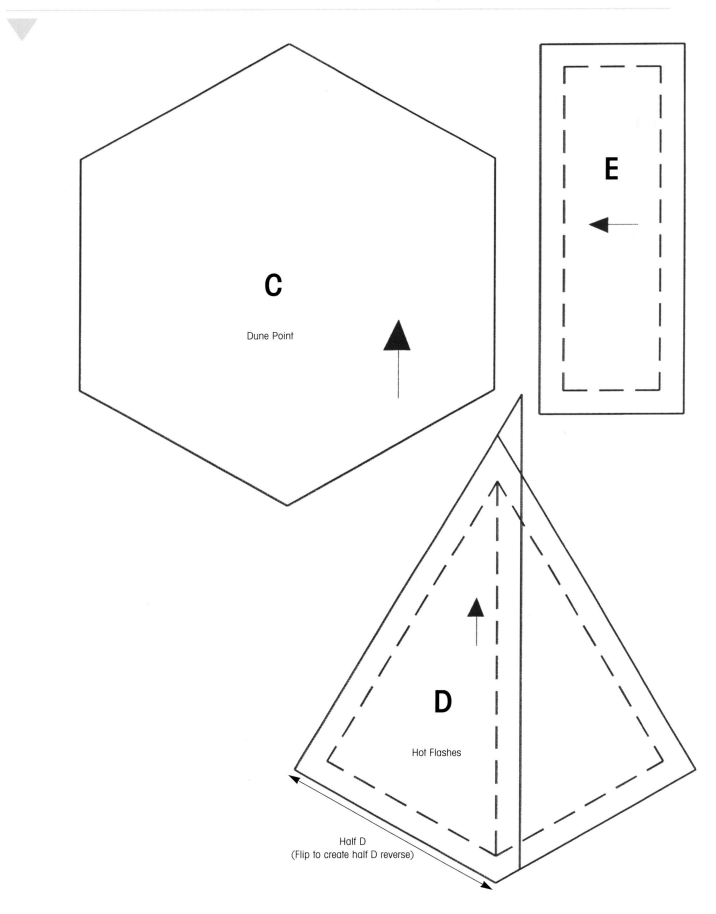

C

Dune Point

E

D

Hot Flashes

Half D
(Flip to create half D reverse)

Wrap Up

I can never decide which part of the quilt-making process I like best: picking the fabric or choosing the design; cutting the fabric or stitching the pieces together; quilting by hand or machine or putting on finishing touches like the binding and name tag. I guess I like the whole process and enjoy each and every part of it while I'm working. However, there are times when everything goes wrong and I'm screaming "This is supposed to be fun?!" No matter—I do persevere. It isn't often that I end up with something that has no redeeming feature. Although, in all honesty, I did once throw out a finished quilt because I thought it was so ugly that I didn't even want to see it around as a blanket for our pets.

Whatever the outcome of our quilts, most of us are quilting because we love the process or at least some part of it. After more than 20 years of quilting, I still marvel at all the new fabrics, the new equipment, the wonderful sewing machines, and the helpful books available to all of us. We've come a long way from haunting thrift shops for cotton (although I still find some treasures there) and rummaging through antique magazines for patterns.

Almost all of us have friends and quilt groups at our fingertips that can help us solve our quilting problems. I'm sure most of us have a quilting buddy or two with whom we can take field trips or share a special quilting moment. I know that not everyone appreciates our enthusiasm. I am especially thankful for my enthusiastic and supportive husband and children. They are always encouraging me and asking about new projects. I'm even lucky enough to have some non-quilting friends who understand my passion and my life's work.

Finishing this book was a lot like wrapping up the details on a huge quilt. It's a good feeling to be able to share some of my techniques with you. I would love to see pictures or slides of what you have done with the patterns and how you have interpreted my designs. You can write to me in care of Quilts, Etc., Prentiss Cove, HCR 64, Box 012, Damariscotta, Maine 04543.

So, have fun making decisions—what pattern, what fabric, what technique, what size. It can be so easy, yet there are times when it can be so complicated. Perhaps because we want to do it all.

And why shouldn't we?

While I am wrapping up this project, I am also thinking about my next project—or perhaps I should say one of my next projects. Whichever one I choose, I plan to enjoy every moment of it, and I hope all the projects you plan turn out as beautifully as you imagined.

Here is to every grand quilt in our future!

Index

Italic numbers indicate photos of quilts

After the Hunt, 2, *110*–114
Australian Seven Sisters, 2, 101–*102*
A Year in the Life of My Tree, 2, 43–48, *44*
    fabric selection and, 43–44

Background
    color selection for, 43–44
    white, 2, 3
Backing, 17
Basic Triangle Quilt, 31–32
Batting, 17
Binding
    attaching, 19–20
    corners, 20
    creating, 18–19
    defined, 18
Blended fabric colors
    A Year in the Life of My Tree, 43–44
    defined, 2
    random color selection, 66–67
    reasons for, 2–3
    softening effect of, 2–3
    trees and, 3
    white background, 3
Blue Dresden Plates, 2, 64, 68–70, *69*
Borders
    cutting, 16
    double, 16
    using Dune Points, 129–130
    for *Pond Lilies,* 96–97
    highlighter, 16, 96–97
    mitering, 80, 97
    notching, 79–80, 97
    piecing and attaching, 54, 97
    second, 97
    with corner block, 108

Contemporary quilts, 43–61
Curved seam sewing, 86–88
Curved triangles, 92–93
Curves, in quilts, 85–98
    assembling 60° Drunkard's Path, 87–88
    Pond Lilies, 92–98
    Whirlwind, 90–91
    Windy Way, 86–89

Design wall, 6
Double border, 16
Drapery fabrics, 22, 34
Dresden Plate quilts
    Blue Dresden Plates, 68–70, *69*
    introduction to, 63–64
    Necktie Quilt, 75–80
    pivot method, 65

Return to Dresden, 71–74
    set-in method, 65
    special techniques used in, 64–65
Drunkard's Path, 85
    assembling 60°, 87–88
Dune Points
    in borders, 129–130
    Pond Lilies and, 98

Fabric
    collecting for quilts, 4–5
    color and random selection of, 66–67
    cutting layered cloth using templates with
        seam allowances, 14
    cutting on grainline, 12–13
    cutting triangle templates with seam
        allowances, 13–14
    drapery, 22, 34
    neckties, 75
    scrap quilts, 5
    selection for, in *A Year in the Life of My
        Tree,* 43–44
    using rotary cutter, 14
Fan quilts
    Green Fans, 66–68
    introduction to, 63–64
    pivot method, 65
    set-in method, 65
    special techniques in, 64–65
Flannel wall, 6
Fly-A-Way, 119–123, *120*
Four-fabric alternate triangle, 24–25
    assembling, 26
Four-fabric triangle, 26
Fractured triangles, 101–114
    After the Hunt, *110*–114
    assembling trees, 112–114
    Hichinin Schimai, *103*–110
    machine paper piecing, 109–110
    separate templates for each fabric
        method, 109
    strip piecing and template method,
        106–109, 112–114

Green Fans, 64, 66–68

Half sets, 24–25
Hichinin Schimai, 2, 3, *103*–110
Highlighter border, 16
    for *Pond Lilies,* 96–97
Hot Flashes, 2, 3, 123–130, *124*

Impressionism, 1
In the ditch, 18
Ironing, 16

Lavender Blue, 49–54

Layout,
    flannel wall and, 6
Lewis, Sara Brown, 63

Machine paper piecing of fractured triangles,
    109–110
Maze, Eva Hoyt, 63
Medallion Quilt
    king, 35–36
    queen, 32–34
Mitered borders, 80
Mitered corners, 20, 52, 80

Necktie Quilt, 64, 75–80
Needles, size of, 17
Notching of border and quilt edge, 79–80, 97

Piecing
    assembling rows, 14–15
    stitching sequence, 15
Pivot method of sewing triangles, 52, 65
Pond Lilies, 16, *92*–98
    borders for, 96–97
    Dune Points and, 98

Quilting, 16–18
    first stitches, 17–18
Quilting frame, using, 17
Quilts
    After the Hunt, 2, *110*–114
    Australian Seven Sisters, 2, 101–*102*
    A Year in the Life of My Tree, 2, 43–48, *44*
    backing, 17
    Basic Triangle Quilt, 31–32
    Blue Dresden Plates, 2, 64, 68–70, <u>*69*</u>
    contemporary, 43–61
    curves in, 85–98
    Dresden Plate, 63–65, 68–80, *69*, *71*
    Fan, 63–66
    Fly-A-Way, 119–123, *120*
    Green Fans, 64, 66–68
    Hichinin Schimai, 2, 3, *103*–110
    Hot Flashes, 12, 3, 123–130, *124*
    impressionistic approach, 1
    Lavender Blue, 49–54
    Medallion Quilt, king, 35–36
    Medallion Quilt, queen, 32–34
    Necktie Quilt, 64, 75–80
    Pond Lilies, 16, *92*–98
    Return to Dresden, 71–74
    Vertical Triangle Quilt, 37–40
    Whirlwind, 90–91
    Windy Way, 6, 86–89

Return to Dresden, 71–74
Reverse half sets, 24–25
Rotary cutter, cutting triangle templates with
    seam allowances, 14
Rows, assembling, 14–15

Scrap quilts, 5
Second border, 97
Set–in method of sewing triangles, 53, 65

Sets, defined, 14
60° triangle. *See* Triangles, 60°
Stars
    45°-triangle, 3, 5
    60°-triangle, 3–4
Stitches
    first quilting stitches, 17–18
    In the ditch, 18
    length of, 18
    walking foot and, 18
Strip piecing and template method of frac-
    tured triangles, 106–109, 112–114

Templates
    for Chapter 4, 41–42
    for Chapter 5, 55–61
    for Chapter 6, 81–83
    for Chapter 7, 99–100
    for Chapter 8, 115–117
    for Chapter 9, 131–132
    fractured triangles and, 106–108
    machine paper piecing, 109–110
    making with no seam allowances, 11
    making with seam allowances, 11–12
    strip piecing and template method,
        106–109, 112–114
Thread, 17
    length of, 18
Trees
    blended fabric colors, 3
    fabric selection and, 43–44
    fractured triangles and, 112–114
Triangles
    curved, 92–93
    four-fabric, 26–27
    four-fabric alternate triangle, 24–25
    fractured, 101–114
    large background, 107–108
    16-fabric, 30
Triangles, 60°
    drawing, 7–10
    enlarging and reducing, 8
    star quilt with, 3–4
    using 1" grid, 8–10
Triangles, 45°
    star quilt with, 3, 5
Triptych I, 2, 22–24
Triptych IV, 2, *24*–27
Triptych XVI, 27–*30*
Triptychs, 21–30
    defined, 21
Turbak, Sue, 43

Vertical Triangle Quilt, 37–40

Walking foot, 18, 19
Wallhanging I, 22–24
Wallhanging IV, 24–27
Wallhanging XVI, 27–30
Whirlwind, 90–91
Windy Way, 6, *86*–89